British Secularism and Religion

Islam, Society and the State

Yahya Birt
Dilwar Hussain
Ataullah Siddiqui
editors

KUBE
PUBLISHING

First published in England by Kube Publishing Ltd,
Markfield Conference Centre
Ratby Lane, Markfield,
Leicestershire LE67 9SY
United Kingdom
Tel: +44 (0) 1530 249230
Fax: +44 (0) 1530 249656
Website: www.kubepublishing.com
Email: info@kubepublishing.com

A Cataloguing-in-Publication data record is available
from the British Library.

ISBN 978-1-84774-015-1 *paperback*

Cover Design: Nasir Cadir
Typesetting: Naiem Qaddoura

Contents

Introduction

~

Predicament or Promise?
Exploring Britain's Unsettled Secularism

Yahya Birt, Dilwar Hussain and Ataullah Siddiqui

It has long been thought that secularism was a settled question in Britain. The overall shape of the institutional arrangements between the established Anglican Church and the state, the steady co-option of post-war Britain's greater religious pluralism, and the widely-held reluctance to invoke God in public debate has lent credibility to the perception that this has indeed been the case. However, since the late 1980s, Britain's secular dispensation has become increasingly unsettled. Although far from being an exclusive contributory factor in our newly unsettled condition, Islam – as Britain's second largest religion – has more often than not served as the lightning rod for this debate. A series of cultural and political crises – from the Satanic Verses Affair, 9/11, 7/7, and the Danish Cartoons crisis, to name only some of the major flashpoints – have served to put the national debate on the public role of religion back on to the centre stage.

Definitional Disputes
We have not set out in this collection to be overly prescriptive with regard to definitional matters. In the academic literature,

and indeed in contemporary public debate in Britain, political, religious or other differences are often played out through definitional disputes themselves. That said, however, there is a broad distinction made between the general historical processes of *secularisation*, and a set of political prescriptions around the relationship between religion and politics, which is often termed as *secularism*.

With regard to secularisation, the sociologist Peter Berger defined it as 'the process by which sectors of society and culture are removed from the domination of religious institutions and symbols' (Berger 1967: 107). By contrast, however, the philosopher Alisdair MacIntyre defines secularisation as 'the transition from beliefs and activities and institutions presupposing beliefs of a traditionally Christian kind to beliefs and activities and institutions of an atheistic kind' (MacIntyre 1967: 7-8). This dichotomy between a naturalised sociological process in Berger's early thought and a more contested, purposeful transformation in MacIntrye's definition reflects the fact that religious traditions may see the framing secular world of communication as their definitional opposite (Bader 2009: 110), and is emblematic of the polarised positions in the discussion. In a more philosophical context, secularism often refers to the understanding that life can be best lived by applying reasoned ethics, and the universe best understood by the process of reasoning, without reference to a deity or other 'supernatural' concepts. Hence there are distinct undertones of atheism or agnosticism (and indeed anti-clericalism) associated with secularism in this sense.

However, the use of the term 'secularism' in this volume is largely focused upon its political sense to refer to the relative separation between state and religion, to non-discrimination among religions and to the guarantees made with respect to the human rights of citizens, regardless of their creed. In his recent work, the philosopher Charles Taylor (2007, 2009) has sought to clarify the meaning of secularism, in a manner that underscores the difficult and contested nature of its definition, and helpfully takes this debate right to the heart of the issues that we think are important to deliberate upon. For instance, he argues that political secularism requires the pursuit of four distinct public goods that are in partial conflict with each other:

1. The exercise of religious freedoms (including the freedom not to believe);
2. The state should not be partial in favour of any one denomination or religion, and within this Taylor does include weak forms of establishment like Britain's, which he regards as largely symbolic and vestigial;
3. Political culture must be inclusive, in Taylor's terms 'fraternal', so that all, including religious groups, are involved in determining society's political identity and how it will achieve a consensus on the distribution of rights and privileges; and
4. Political culture should seek to promote and maintain harmonious relations between all groups, including religious ones.

The definitional dispute about what political secularism means reflects the debate over how these public goods may best be achieved. One view is that these goals may only be achieved if public debate is informed by the exercise of reason alone, a process that requires the strict separation of religion from politics. The other view is that secular democratic politics can, *as a process*, incorporate religious viewpoints within the public sphere, whose character may veer between harmonious relations and agonistic dispute, without harm to these public goods. The second view also assumes that there is sufficient overlap in views to achieve a consensus. Another argument Taylor makes is that insisting on the need to invoke a single higher authority, in this case, pure reason (but equally theocratic rule in a non-secular context) vitiates the fraternal imperatives of inclusion and seeking harmony in political culture. The usefulness of Taylor's four-part definition lies in the fact that it highlights the delicate balance required to uphold religious freedoms, state impartiality between religions, the principle of inclusivity and the aspiration to seek greater political cohesion simultaneously.

It will be noted that while Abdullah Sahin in Chapter 1 and Tariq Modood in Chapter 5 employ slightly different terms in their definitional discussions, they are both largely concerned to get at a difference between an ideological rigidity that seeks in some manner to exclude religion or marginalise it in ways that are unjust from the secular democratic public sphere and a more accommodative ethos that allows a public role for religion. Sahin defines the former as *secularism* or 'an ideological position that confines faith strictly to the personal sphere of life' and the latter as *secularity* or 'a political principle integral to democratic inclusion, may accommodate ... the diversity of cultures, value systems and faith traditions that make up modern plural society'. Similarly, Modood proposes a spectrum for *secularism*, which he defines as a 'religion–politics separationist view, which is clearly normative rather than scientific, can take quite different forms, either as an idea or as practice and can be more or less restrictive', which he argues may take radical or moderate (or accommodative) forms. Nick Spencer in Chapter 2 also notes the underlying similarity in the distinction the incumbent Archbishop of Canterbury Rowan Williams makes between *programmatic* and *procedural* secularism. Ted Cantle in Chapter 6 accepts the fact of a diverse society with the participation of religious voices in public life, but insists upon the rational and evidential basis of governmental policymaking, so making a secular distinction between public debate and policymaking.

Secularism in Practice – The British Case in Comparative Perspective

In terms of political practice, as opposed to theory, secularism has taken on many different forms of governance. However, the rationale of secularism that finds its roots in Enlightenment values as well as the desire to rid Europe of religious conflict and tension tends to dominate the debate. In this spirit it is assumed that the public arena ought to be free of religious interference. Religious believers, and, at the present juncture Muslims in particular, are often seen to be 'disturbing' the steady state of British secularism by reminding Britain of the medieval past that she wishes to leave behind. However, both of these assumptions – that the public arena was ever really free from religion or that there was a steady state prior to Muslim migration to post-war Britain – do not bear up to critical examination, and we would like to suggest that it would be more useful to start the debate from an analysis of *actually-existing secularisms*, in which the British tradition of secularism forms but one instance.

The most important historical fact has been the long continuity of England's constitutional arrangements for the relationship between Church and State: no triumphant invasion since 1066, a reformation in the sixteenth century that put the English monarch in place of the Pope at the head of the Church, and a civil war in the seventeenth century that restored the monarchy but was defined by a political culture of republicanism. This has profoundly marked the English sense of secularism as one that has avoided the revolutionary root-and-branch reform of, say, France and America, in favour of piecemeal reform leaving many timeworn and archaic features in place. In fact there has been a marked preference for preserving the increasingly symbolic aspects of England as a confessional state, even if social, political and religious change has meant that reform has never been abandoned either; in short, the English model of secularism has been informed by an ethic of pragmatic gradualism that pays due attention to the dialectic between symbolic authority and the realities of social and political change.

Thus since 1689 the Protestant nature of the monarchy has been insisted upon: the monarch must be Protestant and cannot marry a Catholic; however, while the monarch is the Supreme Governor of the Church of England, he or she has been obliged since 1707 to swear to support the Presbyterian Church of Scotland, which retains its formal independence.[1] Thus, in constitutional terms, Scotland is more formally secular than England. Furthermore there were two formal disestablishments of the Churches of Ireland (1871) and of Wales (1920), but these were not precursors to disestablishment in England, but were the outcome of regional conditions of the period. All this is indicative of how traditions of continuity and gradual piecemeal reform have led to a multiplicity of Church–State arrangements within the four nations of the United Kingdom today (Morris 2009).

There is not the space here to provide a comprehensive historical reflection upon the tests of legitimacy that these arrangements have faced, but instead to note that since 1945 there have been two main challenges: (i) the emergence of a post-Christian society and, with the great post-war migrations, (ii) a higher degree of religious pluralism, both Christian and non-Christian, than in the past. That there has been an increased rate of decline in worship and participation in Christian rites of passage since the 1960s (Brown 2000) has obvious salience for the symbolic legitimacy of the English confessional state, but an exploration of the implications of the changing nature of identification with Christianity in Britain is not the main aim of this volume. Perhaps the major sociological outcome, however, has been a marked deinstitutionalisation of religious expression or a condition of 'believing without belonging' (Davie 1994). The chief reason for our inattention is that the locus of the debate on the merits or demerits of the Church of England's continued establishment has largely been within the Church itself. As a corollary to that, the non-Christian religious minorities have largely been content to support continued establishment on the basis that some representation of religion within the state is better than

---

[1] In 1994, the current heir to the Throne, the Prince of Wales, floated the idea that the Monarch's title 'Defender of the Faith' ought to more accurately reflect both the nation's greater religious pluralism and the ostensive sense of the original Latin title – *Fidei Defensor* – by being amended to 'Defender of Faith'.

none, although whether the Church of England should act as an effective proxy for religious minorities that have preferred to treat directly with the state has been more contentious (Modood 1997: 3-15).

The focus, however, in this volume has been drawn more towards the implications of the second main development in post-war Britain, which is the emergence of a far greater degree of multi-faith pluralism. The 2001 Census showed that 72% defined themselves as 'Christian', 23% as having 'no faith' or not having entered a category at all, and the other 5% belonging to non-Christian religions, half of whom are Muslims; in short, the debate on revisiting British traditions of secularism is likely to reflect the fact that British society is now 'three-dimensional' – Christian, secular and religiously plural (Walker 2008: 52).

Although the contributors examine particular aspects of British secularism, it is appropriate to offer a brief outline of its basic features in comparison with America and France. Britain is often conceived of possessing a tradition of moderate secularism with an Anglican establishment that has encouraged a shift towards multi-faith inclusion. France and America unlike Britain have a formal separation between religion and state. However, their political cultures could not be more different. Religion in American civil society is strong and has influenced politics directly, while in France it is relatively weak and has furthermore been actively discouraged by the state as a form of divisive communitarianism. However the French prefer to regulate religion from the top downwards by conferring institutional legal status on religions and denominations, including Islam;[2]

---

[2] The tension inherent in the French model lies in the fact that republicanism struggles with the impulse to order and control public religion politically, either by asserting the supremacy of the state over religion by intervening in theological matters or by asserting the national autonomy or 'Frenchness' of religions from foreign control or by asserting both, and the need to avoid entangling the secular state in religious matters. Conversely, upholding non-interference in religious life and institutions as an absolute principle might lead to a loss of state control. See Roy (2007) for a fuller discussion, especially pp. 25-8.

while the British prefer to encourage religious interest groups to coalesce and to work together for certain common goods with the Church of England, a process which has arguably led to something akin to an informal multi-faith establishment. In Britain and France, political culture has often frowned upon open religious discourse, whereas in America, it has often been accepted as integral to its democratic culture. Nearly all of our contributors reflect on the uniqueness of the British model of secularism in comparison with its French and American counterparts; Tariq Modood in Chapter 5 argues further that the British accommodationist or moderate model of secularism should be accorded a normative status not only because of its reasonableness but because it is broadly similar to the model of secularism developed in North-Western Europe.

Our Approach

This collection is the outcome of a seminar 'British Muslims and the Secular State', which was hosted by the Policy Research Centre at the Islamic Foundation and the Markfield Institute of Higher Education in London in January 2009. Originally our intention as editors was to take a fourfold approach. Firstly, we sought to deliberate upon secularism and public religion through a focus upon the Muslim minority context in Britain as it impinges upon the question of faith in a secular context, while acknowledging the overall impact of the debate about religion and politics in Muslim-majority contexts. Secondly, we were concerned to take an interdisciplinary approach to create a fruitful synergy between theological approaches and political science, as it is crucial that normative theological approaches should be thoroughly informed by systematic analyses of the lived context from the academic and policy worlds, and that political science should at least be more theologically aware when discussing the role of public religion. To this end, the range of seminar partici-pants reflected a range of backgrounds from academia, activism, interfaith, policymaking and politics in order that general reflections should be grounded in concrete concerns and everyday experience. Thirdly, we were equally concerned to avoid another common form of compartmentalisation, which is to look at secularism from the viewpoint of one faith community only, or indeed from any particular orientation towards secularism itself. Therefore the discussion was framed in a 'multilogical' manner as it seemed obvious to us that both the seminar and the book should naturally reflect the fact that this is a wide-ranging, national debate, where criticisms, reflections, mooted solutions and so on should be aired publicly and deliberated upon collectively. Finally all these strands had to be considered with due attention to the concrete British context rather than to some abstract definition of what secularism is or ought to be, for, as editors, we share the conviction that both analysis and recommendations are best framed in a grounded and realistic manner.

However, as is often the case with open-ended 'multilogical' discussions, the final book has taken on a broader shape than was originally intended for although Islam has often been a catalyst for current deliberation on the British tradition of secularism, nearly all our contributors were concerned not to single Islam out but to reflect critically and more generally upon religion and secularism in the British experience. Thus the final form of this volume is somewhat of a hybrid for while there is a focus on Islam theologically and upon issues around religion and the secular state with reference to British Muslim communities, Islam is by no means exclusively the sole object of attention.

The Muslim Debate on Secularism in the Majority and Minority Contexts

In recent times Muslims have approached the issue of secularism from a distinct historical experience. They have often – but not always – taken their point of departure from anti-colonial movements that have sought to, or placed a high value upon, restoring the caliphate as a symbol of Muslim unity, that looked back to Muslim history for inspiration and have created nostalgic and romanticised associations between the state and religious authority while appropriating modern political ideologies in the process (Al-Azmeh 1993). It has not been uncommon to hear the argument in the post-colonial period that Islam does not recognise a division between the temporal and transcendental.

Moreover, it should be noted that the lived Muslim experience of the interaction between religion and politics over the last century has often been far from pleasant. Olivier Roy's thesis (1994) of the 'failure of political Islam' seems to have been borne out by recent experience if we consider soberly the situation of despotism and authoritarianism in the Muslim world, including the various states that have been created and fashioned in the name of Islam. All of this has meant that while some have strongly advocated a closer and stronger relationship between religion and politics, the Muslim journey for others has been a search for how to limit the power and influence of authoritarian religion.

Therefore a more discerning and critical look at Muslim history under the aegis of the fact that Britain's secular democracy is *the* framing context for political participation, whether faith-inspired or otherwise, would suggest that a far more open-minded and self-critical reflection is urgently required. In this respect, Abdullah Sahin makes a timely and important intervention in Chapter 1 that we do not wish to pre-empt here, except to comment briefly upon the context and nature of the intra-Muslim debate on secularism in the minority context.

It is important to acknowledge that early Islamic thought, which developed during the period of great territorial expansion in Asia and Africa under a unified caliphate, the notion of the Muslim living as part of a minority held an exceptional status, as a deviation from the norm of majority Muslim societies, under which the codes of *shari'a* (consisting of Islamic law, ethics and morals) would hold sway. One of the major legal schools, the Malikis, prohibited any form of residence in non-Muslim lands while the others tended to allow it as an exception, seeing it as carrying dangers of assimilation, strengthening 'the enemy' or vitiating what they saw as the superiority of Islam over other religions (Abou El Fadl 1994: 134-5). Thus Muslim residence in non-Muslim lands was articulated in the form of legal exceptionalism, and minority status was not viewed as a permanent state of affairs. Legal dispensations (*rukhus*) were often granted to ameliorate conditions of difficulty or even duress.

In the past, the debate about the minority context was predicated on a straightforward legal dichotomy between the land of Islam (*dar al-islam*) and the land of unbelief (*dar al-kufr*), a division that presumed the world of pre-modern empire, a world of mobile frontiers rather than fixed borders. The disempowered Muslim minority represented a temporary lapse from what was considered the default status of the protection and power of Muslim rule. But European colonialism decisively invalidated that presumption. At one point, around 1920, that presumption was almost completely reversed: more than 90% of Muslims were under direct or indirect European rule, and for many, the ideal of the secular was imposed at this point, as a hallmark of civilisation and progress. Subsequently, Muslim nation-states gained independence from Egypt in 1922 to the independence of Kosovo in 2008, and have experimented with various modern political ideologies and modalities including nationalism, constitutionalism, authoritarianism, socialism, Marxism, fascism, democracy, liberalism, Islamism and so on, which have all construed the 'secular' as anything from liberation to enslavement. The two most influential post-colonial political models in the Muslim world, almost in the form of thesis and antithesis, have been the Turkish Revolution and the abolition of the caliphate (1920-4) and the emergence of the most durable modern Islamic republic during the Iranian Revolution (1979). The legacy of that 'forcible conscription into modernity' to use Talal Asad's description, of which European-style secularism was an integral part, and its long post-colonial aftermath, marked by the Arab defeat at the hands of Israel in 1967, should neither be ignored nor should it remain sacrosanct and unquestioned given the very different and legitimate aspirations of British Muslims today.

Contemporary Muslim theological discussion of 'the secular' is all too often largely, if not exclusively, framed within the terms of this reaction to European colonialism. Secularism is largely equated with the progressive and forcible imposition of atheism, whereby the modern state actively seeks to marginalise religion, institutionally and intellectually. Often, therefore, the response to secularism has been highly antagonistic, and stated in trenchant creedal terms. Secularism is considered to entail the very 'absence of religion' and therefore an authentic modern version of an Islamic polity cannot by definition be a secular democracy. Islam is considered to be a comprehensive and immutable ideology and so there is no room for state reform as such. Islam and secularism stand in stark opposition to each other: Islam is religion and secularism is the absence of religion and atheism. Although some of these trenchant critics have recognised a distinction between atheism and secularism, with secularism as the separation of religion and state, the latter is characterised in its entirety as being so anti-religion as to elide any meaningful distinction with atheism. Others even include the process of secularisation with secularism as being part of a closed ideology that is inimical to Islam (Al-Attas 1993, Masud 2005, Nasr 1996: 80-106, Qaradawi 1981).

Within the Western context, the implications of this anti-secularist trend among Muslim minorities has retained some influence in construing minority status as a temporary and passing state of affairs, prioritizing the need to establish an Islamic political order, and in downplaying alternative medieval and modern interpretations that have legitimised non-Muslim political orders as Islamic if they uphold basic religious and political freedoms (Masud 1989). It is noticeable in fact that this latter interpretation has become much more prevalent among Western Muslims over the last 20 years (Darsh 1992, Hellyer 2007, Ramadan 2004, Suleiman 2009). In short, it is our contention that the classical anti-colonial and later post-colonial anti-secularist positions have largely ignored or misconstrued how *actually-existing secularisms* operate in Europe and elsewhere, and it is our hope that Muslim theological reflection undertakes the conscientious effort to start from the contextual reality of 'the secular' to be found on the ground.

All this preamble is merely to say that we recognise that any discussion of 'the secular' and what it means for British Muslims with regard to the political dimensions of their minority status cannot be easily divorced from the wider question as to what role the secular division between religion and politics does or might ideally play in Muslim majority societies. This is particularly true of the theological dimension because it is as essential to discuss the fundamental category of the 'secular' itself and not to confine the discussion to its second-order entailments like tolerance, human rights and freedom, important as these entailments might be. In other words, Muslims are bound to return to the same fundamental questions about the role of faith in public life whatever the nature of their context. However, while recognising that we cannot avoid fundamental questions about the relationship between politics and religion, which are ably covered by Abdullah Sahin in Chapters 1 and 4, of which the most central is the political implication of the relationship between Divine sovereignty and human agency and moral responsibility in the world, we would stress that the focus of our discussion inevitably remains the British context.

Going beyond the critical theory of secularism

Given our preference for a 'multilogical' and interdisciplinary approach, it might well be pointed out that we have not done justice to the burgeoning critical literature on the shortcomings of liberal democratic secularism with regard to its treatment of religious groups.[3] It is beyond the remit of this introduction to attempt to survey this literature here, but, using one of the leading figures in this debate, the anthropologist Talal Asad, as a foil, we will note its limitations for our purposes here.

The first limitation is that Asad aims to parochialise the epistemic category of the secular and the political doctrine of secularism as universalising norms by pointing to their European and Christian origins between the sixteenth and the nineteenth centuries. His insight that religion and the secular emerge together with the secular defining religion in such a way as to privilege liberal Protestant assumptions about private belief constituting religion's essence is surely important for understanding the strictures that colonial modernity and indeed post-colonial Europe have laid upon non-Christian religions. In particular it helps us to understand why embodied ritual religious practices, such as the *hijab* (the headscarf), may be singled out under aggressive secularisms (Asad 1993, 2003, Bowen 2007, Scott 2007). And yet, while Asad would not deny that there were pre-modern precursors in medieval Islamdom and Christendom for the separation of religious and secular instruments of government, these are merely noted. However, Asad's emphasis runs against any attempt at ethical realism on the part of British Muslims who may legitimately seek (i) to argue for those forms of liberal secularism that work better for religious minorities,[4] and, in so doing, (ii) to assess the fruitful

---

[3] E.g., Audi and Wolterstorff (1997), Bader (2007), Bowen (2007, 2010), Brown (2006), Connelly (1999), Eberle (2002), Hurd (2008), March (2009), Scott (2007), Smith (2010), Sullivan (2005), Swaine (2006), and Weithman (2002).

[4] Asad has occasionally indicated a preference for ethical realism, or an accommodative approach, but it does run against the thrust of his work: 'this process does not ... require a principled reference by the state to "the proper place of religion" in a secular society – any more than it needs to have a principled reference to "the proper place" of *anything*. ... [O]ne may resist the temptation to "defend secularism" or "attack civic religion". One might instead learn to argue about the best ways of supporting particular liberties while limiting others, of minimising social and individual harm. In brief, one might commit oneself with assessing particular demands and threats without have to confront the *general* "danger of religion".' (Asad 2006: 526)

indications within Islamic intellectual history that the relative autonomy of powers, e.g. of law from politics, provides in this debate, rather than assuming that it must be inauthentic and foreign (Ahmad 2009: 15-16, Bangstad 2009, Moosa 2009, Sahin, this volume, Strenski 2010: 42-46). In fact, for some critics the project of such an ethical realism would be seen as cultural and intellectual capitulation (Mahmood 2006).

The second difficulty in Asad's work flows from the first, which is that the categories of 'the West' and 'the non-West' serve as an organising dyad that determines how non-Westerners are perceived and whom are therefore in a sense constituted by the West through its historic and contemporary power and domination. Authenticity, therefore, for non-Westerners is construed largely in terms of resisting this categorisation to find legitimacy in tradition, or, in the case of Muslims, Islam (Bangstad 2009). Indeed as one commentator has noted:

> Instead of being the backward other of European modernity, Islam may now be taken up as the pious other of secularism, the resisting other of neo-colonialism.... Elevated to such a position of significant alterity, the religious traditions of Muslims gain particular brilliance and importance for the sake of highlighting their particularity through their difference. (Schielke 2010)

This role of 'significant alterity' also surfaces in Asad's gloomy and pessimistic reading of the place of Muslim minorities as being fated to be *in* but not *of* Europe, for 'it [is] difficult if not impossible to represent Muslims as Muslims' (2003: 173). Yet while it would certainly be remiss to be naïve about the worrying rise of anti-Muslim politics in Europe today, millions of European Muslims have not abandoned the hope of being Muslims *of* Europe. In short, in Asad's work it appears that the figure of the Muslim is cast as a Grand Inquisitor (Werbner 2005) who is ready to pass final judgement on the failures of secular liberalism: a stance that plays all too well into the more self-defeating forms of Muslim identity politics to be found in Britain and Europe today.

Interdisciplinary Approaches

The book is arranged into two strands – theological and political – which in our view are too often kept apart, to the detriment of both. It is our hope that such strands can be drawn together for the mutual enrichment of the discussion. Keeping them separate has demonstrably allowed for some persistent stereotypes to persist. We have already given the example of how some Muslim intellectuals have reduced secularism to little more than the aggressive promotion of atheism, with little consideration of the facts on the ground that face British Muslims today.

We remain unconvinced that there is any utility in holding discussions about religion and politics in Britain today in isolation. Islam and the rise of multi-faith Britain has had, for good or ill, a major impact upon what were seen as settled questions about the relationship between religion and the state in Britain. These are quite obviously issues that affect us all and therefore it seems that a 'multilogical' approach suggests itself if we are to search successfully for new answers together and in common. This approach would seem to militate against more partial or self-serving agendas. We recognise too that the multi-faith discussion in the British context is wider than that between the Abrahamic faiths, including obviously no-faith and the other world religions that are part of an evolving multi-faith establishment in Britain.

Another common stereotype among some Western political theorists and policymakers is one of a monolithic Islam, or, more generally, fundamentalist monotheism, which is set up as a bogeyman against which they may positively highlight their core values and institutional arrangements, often in an ideal-ised form. More seriously this kind of argument has had legal and policy implications, and has led to what Tariq Modood has called a panicky retreat to a public–private distinction by which religio-political claims made by Muslims cannot be accommodated, should not be recognised and should remain prescriptively private. These claims may be characterised as exceptional, unreasonable demands rather than as claims to even-handed treatment or public recognition. This even includes, in some sections of the British press, the invention of concessions to phantom Muslim demands, e.g. the promotion of Winterval festivals by local councils as opposed to Christmas. In short, the debate about Muslims and 'the secular' is often therefore the victim of clashing stereotypes, pitting idealisations of ourselves against each other, rather than dealing methodically with each point of conflict as it arises, case by case.

In Chapter 1, Abdullah Sahin sets out to engage critically and creatively from the Islamic tradition of political theology with what he terms as 'secularity', an accommodative arrangement that does not exclude religion from public life and that is committed to democratic inclusion. He is critical not only of 'secularism' that systematically excludes religion from public life, but also of reactionary traditional trends among Muslims that came out of the colonial experience. Instead what is needed is a mutual culture of 'critical openness', an approach for which he finds classical antecedents in Ibn Taymiyya and Najm al-Din al-Tufi.

Nick Spencer and Norman Solomon in Chapters 2 and 3 largely endorse Sahin's distinction between secularity and secularism from Christian and Jewish perspectives respectively. Nick Spencer reminds us that whatever the shortcomings of secular democracies like Britain, such as the attempt to diminish religious voices in public debate over contentious issues like abortion, e.g. through overly-prescriptive definitions of what ought to constitute proper public reason, we would do well to remember the coercive secularism of twentieth-century totalitarian states like the Soviet Union that quashed religious freedoms in the name of progress.

Norman Solomon does warn that religious groups should no longer expect special privileges but only the normal access to public life that should be open to any other grouping. They ought to consider too that where established scientific facts are central to public debate they cannot be ignored. Solomon remarks that the real clash is not between Islam and the West but between the religions and their response to secular modernity; he is in agreement with Sahin that creative engagement is much preferable to a reactionary retreat into tradition. With the advent of modernity, political absolutism and religious authority have been fundamentally challenged but the response to this challenge should be not reactionary in spirit, which has been manifested in gender inequality for instance. However in the creative response to modernity, religion should not be reduced to values alone, but rather its 'laws, rituals, history, legends, spiritual exercises' and its whole vocabulary of faithfulness should be retained.

In his rejoinder to Spencer and Solomon, Sahin largely agrees that with engagement there remain the dangers of political exclusion of Muslims and a growth in the narrative of Muslim victimhood that stymies taking due responsibility for policy issues, e.g. over extremism, but Sahin, following Jürgen Habermas, disagrees that the secular public sphere need be dominated solely by scientific rationality when it may easily draw upon other civilizational and humanistic traditions to inform its working.

In the second part of the book, Tariq Modood makes a powerful case in Chapter 5 that Britain's (and North-Western Europe's) moderate and accommodative secularism should be appreciated more widely than has been the case in the past, both in terms of liberal political theory and as an historical and contemporary fact on the ground. And considering that this form of secularism does not preclude religion–state connections, Modood then goes on to enumerate five reasons why the secular state should be interested in public religion: (i) the truth of religious claims made, subject to robust democratic processes, in policymaking, if not as a basis for a secular democratic state; (ii) the judicious control of violent religious fanaticism; (iii) the social and moral benefits of religious lifestyles upon society; (iv) the recognition of religious identity as a basis for participative citizenship at the levels of individual, minority group and national belonging; and (v) respect for religion as a cultural, historical or civilizational public good.

Ted Cantle in Chapter 6 argues for a sharp distinction between Britain's increasingly plural religious society and the rational secular basis for governance and policymaking. The former should be protected by upholding the principles of non-discrimination by the state, which entails disestablishment in his view, and of personal religious conscience in matters like religious dress. While religious values may inform public deliberation, the secular democratic state should remain an arbiter between competing religious or other factions and its ultimate mode and frame of reference should be rational decision-making based upon factual evidence.

In Chapter 7, Sunder Katwala, while recognising the strengths of Britain's accommodative secularism, is more sceptical that Britain can continue to muddle along with the status quo given how contentious the role of public religion has become. He suggests that a new settlement must be underpinned by fundamental human rights and that any more formal co-establishment of multi-faith Britain has to be negotiated in some shape or form, a process in which the Church of England may still be able to play a brokering role. This new settlement would have to be hammered out through public debate to have proper legitimacy. Attention should be given to the dignified aspects of the constitution such as reinventing the coronation ceremony in multi-faith terms. While the liberal state should never impede any pursuit of the good (including the religious) life, and may even support it as it does heritage and high culture, it should draw clear lines of principle around freedom of speech and offence, the right to exit religion and so on. Katwala ends by suggesting that any new settlement will depend upon the 'excluded middle' of religious and non-religious moderates prevailing over the contemporary 'culture war' between secularism and faith in Britain.

In his response to Cantle, Modood argues in Chapter 8 that it is wrongheaded to assume that (i) beliefs cannot be reasoned about or challenged or that (ii) reason itself does not precede from fundamental values or worldviews, religious or non-religious; in other words, it is misleading to characterise secular governance, law-making or policy as being primarily determined by empiricism and science alone. He also elaborates further his argument that the accommodative form of secularism should be not regarded as 'incomplete' by Katwala, for what characterises moderate or accommodative secularism, as Alfred Stepan puts it, is that it respects the mutual autonomy of politics and religion through 'twin tolerations', and so it should therefore be seen as central to liberal democracy. Modood also contests Cantle's view that disestablishment in a plural democratic society such as ours should be seen as 'inevitable' or that it would necessarily provide a ready-made solution as the evidence from the United States is that strict separation does not end religion–state conflict.

In her Afterword, Maleiha Malik cautions against an undue optimism that goodwill and the accommodative spirit of British secularism will prove sufficient to avoid all ongoing or future conflict, even if 'negotiation, mediation and compromise', which may take legal or non-legal forms, remains the most effective way forward. Firstly Malik warns against focusing too much upon Islam when changed expectations now pose challenges to all the major religions, e.g. the priority now given to equality in gender relations and sexual orientation over the exercise of religious conscience. Secondly, while it is important that some Muslims may seek various forms of rapprochement between Islamic political theology and secular democracy, the British secular state should not neglect the rights of those Muslims whom, while choosing a path of rejection, remain law-abiding citizens. In any case, contemporary Islamic thought could itself accommodate a number of possible positions on any new secular settlement, including either multi-faith co-option within Anglican establishment or disestablishment to undergird non-discrimination between all religions and the State. Finally, she notes that for British secularism to be truly accommodative, it should address social, economic and political disadvantage where that pertains to marginalised religious minorities to enable rather than disable full public participation.

Finally, all our contributors deserve thanks for their willingness to write in a multilogical format, and we would like thank all of our seminar participants – Sughra Ahmad, Sheikh Saeed Bahmanpour, Andrew Copson, Dr Harriet Crabtree, Dr David Green, Professor Gwen Griffith-Dickson, Dr Usama Hasan, Professor Michael Kenny, Dr Brian Klug, Dr Patrick Riordan and Navid Siddiqi for their lively, sustained and critical input – but of course we and our contributors alone are responsible for the views expressed in this volume. We would like to end by acknowledging the active support and aid of Haris Ahmed, Samina Ali, Irshad Baqui, Nasir Cadir, Naiem Qaddoura and Abdullah Sahin in putting the seminar and the publication together.

References

Abou El Fadl, K. (1994) 'Legal debates on Muslim minorities: between rejection and accommodation', *Journal of Religion and Ethics*, 22: 127-62.

Ahmad, I. (2009) *Islamism and Democracy in India* (Princeton: University Press).

Asad, T. (1993) *Genealogies of Religion* (Baltimore, MD: John Hopkins University Press).

––– (2003) *Formations of the Secular* (Stanford, CA: Stanford University Press).

––– (2006) 'Trying to Understand French Secularism' in H. de Vries and L.E. Sullivan (eds.) *Political Theologies* (New York: Fordham University Press), pp. 494-526.

Al-Attas, M.N. (1993) *Islam and Secularism* (Kuala Lumpur: International Institute of Islamic Thought and Civilisation).

Audi, R. and N. Wolterstorff (1997) *Religion in the Public Square* (Lanham, MD: Rowman & Littlefield).

Al-Azmeh, A. (1993) *Islams and Modernities* (London: Verso).

Bader, V. (2007) *Secularism or Democracy?* (Amsterdam: University Press).

——— (2009) 'Secularism, public reason or moderately agonistic democracy?' in G.B. Levey and T. Modood (eds.), pp. 110-35.

Bangstad, S. (2009) 'Contesting secularism/s: Secularism and Islam in the work of Talal Asad', *Anthropological Theory*, 9/2: 188-208.

Berger, P.L. (1967) *The Sacred Canopy* (New York: Doubleday).

Bowen, J.R. (2007) *Why the French don't like headscarves* (Princeton: University Press).

——— (2010) *Can Islam be French?* (Princeton: University Press).

Brown, C.G. (2000) *The Death of Christian Britain* (London: Routledge).

Brown, W. (2006) *Regulating Aversion* (Princeton: University Press).

Connelly, W.E. (1999) *Why I am not a Secularist* (Minneapolis: Minnesota University Press).

Davie, G. (1994) *Religion in Britain since 1945* (Oxford: Blackwell).

Darsh, S.M. (1992) *Muslims in the West: A Fiqh Seminar in France* (London: n.p.).

Eberle, C.J. (2002) *Religious Conviction in Liberal Politics* (Cambridge: University Press).

Hellyer, H.A. (2007) 'Minorities, Muslims and Shari'a: Some Reflections on Islamic Law and Muslims without Political Power', *Islam and Christian-Muslim Relations*, 18/1: 85-109.

Hurd, E.S. (2008) *The Politics of Secularism in International Relations* (Princeton: University Press).

Levey, G.B. and T. Modood (eds.) (2009) *Secularism, Religion and Multicultural Citizenship* (Cambridge: University Press).

MacIntyre, A. (1967) *Secularization and Moral Change* (Oxford: University Press).

Mahmood, S. (2006) 'Secularism, Hermeneutics, Empire: The Politics of Islamic Reformation', *Public Culture*, 18/2: 323-47.

March, A.F. (2009) *Islam and Liberal Citizenship* (New York: Oxford University Press).

Masud, M.K. (1989) 'Being Muslim in a Non-Muslim Polity: Three Alternative Models', *Journal of the Institute of Muslim Minority Affairs*, 10/1: 118-28.

––– (2005) 'The Construction and Deconstruction of Secularism as an Ideology in Contemporary Muslim Thought', *Asian Journal of Social Science*, 33/3: 363-83.

Modood, T. (ed.) (1997) *Church, State and Religious Minorities* (London: Policy Studies Institute).

Moosa, E. (2009) Personal email communication with Y. Birt, 22nd May.

Morris, R.M. (ed.) (2009) *Church and State in 21st Century Britain* (New York: Palgrave MacMillan).

Nasr, S.V.R. (1996) *Mawdudi and the Making of Islamic Revivalism* (New York: Oxford University Press).

Al-Qaradawi, Y. (1981) *Al-Islam wa al-'Almaniyyah Waghan li Wagh* (Cairo, n.p.).

Ramadan, T. (2004) *Western Muslims and the Future of Islam* (New York: Oxford University Press).

Roy, O. (1994) *The Failure of Political Islam* (Cambridge, Mass.: Harvard University Press).

––– (2007) *Secularism confronts Islam*, trans. by G. Holoch (New York: Columbia University Press).

Schielke, S. (2010), 'Second thoughts about the anthropology of Islam, or how to make sense of grand schemes in everyday life', conference presentation, Zentrum Moderner Orient, Berlin, June.

Scott, J.W. (2007) *The Politics of the Veil* (Princeton: University Press).

Smith, S.D. (2010) *The Disenchantment of Secular Discourse* (Harvard: University Press).

Strenski, I. (2010) *Why Politics can't be freed from Religion* (Oxford: Blackwell).

Suleiman, Y. (2009) *Contextualising Islam in Britain* (Cambridge: University Press).

Sullivan, W.F. (2005) *The Impossibility of Religious Freedom* (Princeton: University Press).

Swaine, L. (2006) *The Liberal Conscience* (New York: Columbia University Press).

Taylor, C. (2007) *A Secular Age* (Harvard: Belknap).

––– (2009) 'What is Secularism?' in G.B. Levey and T. Modood (eds.), pp. xi-xxii.

Walker, P. (2008) *Religious Diversity in the UK* (London: Continuum).

Werbner, P. (2005) 'Islamophobia: Incitement to Religious Hatred – Legislating for a New Fear?' *Anthropology Today*, 21/1: 5-9.

Weithman, P.J. (2002) *Religion and the Obligations of Citizenship* (Cambridge: University Press).

Part I

Theological Perspectives

Part 1

Theological Perspectives

Chapter 1

∼

Islam, Secularity and the Culture of Critical Openness
A Muslim Theological Reflection

Abdullah Sahin

This chapter attempts to develop an Islamic perspective on contemporary Western democratic secularity in which diverse Muslim communities constitute an important part of its religious and cultural plurality. After a discussion of the historical and contemporary dynamics that inform today's Muslim self-understanding, the chapter argues for a new Muslim culture of engagement to develop Islamically-meaningful responses to the challenges posed by secular modernity. The chapter further argues that *secularity*, defined here as a political principle integral to democratic inclusion, may accommodate – in a just manner – the diversity of cultures, value systems and faith traditions that make up modern plural society. On the other hand, it is argued that *secularism*, defined here as an ideological position that confines faith strictly to the personal sphere of life, neither reflects the reality of contemporary Western societies nor is compatible with Islam. By exploring the political theology of Islam, I argue that while secularism thus defined remains incompatible with Islam, secularity as democratic inclusion does not necessarily

3

conflict with Islamic teachings. The chapter develops the position that Muslim social and legal theory should remain central to a serious reflection on Islam and secularity – particularly with reference to the principle of the common or public good (*maslaha*), and the fundamental hermeneutic strategy underpinning it, namely, that of discerning the intent and projected horizon of wider meanings behind the Divine Will (*maqasid* and *ta'lil al-ahkam*). My overall argument is that *critical openness*, a necessary precondition for meaningful dialogue within multi-cultural societies, requires that Muslim communities reassess their role in secular democratic politics in terms of their faith tradition. Similarly, critical openness also entails that, in its encounter with non-Western faith traditions, the modalities of the accommodation that the secular state makes should be carefully reconsidered.

Towards a Muslim culture of engagement

There are several interrelated historical and contemporary dynamics that inform the diversity of Muslim self-expression today. The Muslim tradition is an *internal* dynamic guiding the lives of many Muslims in the modern world. This tradition contains layers of historically-contingent interpretation and appropriation of core Muslim values that are cumulatively derived from the Qur'an and Prophetic tradition (*sunna*). A major *external* dynamic influencing contemporary Muslim self-understanding is what was once known as the struggle between 'Islamdom' and 'Christendom', which, after a profound secularisation process, has come to be termed as the 'Islam–West conflict'. Furthermore, these dynamics came to be mediated by the rise of national and transnational Muslim movements of political resistance and religious renewal that have played a significant role in the formation of contemporary Muslim identity politics. It should be noted that the radicalism in the religious discourses of these movements has been shaped by their strong opposition to European colonisation of the Muslim world, the effects of subsequent decolonisation, the democratic deficit in many Muslim societies, and the current round of proxy and direct military interventions in the Muslim world. This radicalism has in turn resulted in the emergence of European-style nation-states without, in many cases, the accompaniment of a robust indigenous secular and democratic political culture. More recently, the terrorist attacks of 9/11 and 7/7 among others, as well as the ongoing conflict in the Middle East, have also significantly shaped how Muslims see themselves and how they are perceived in today's increasingly globalised world.

The spectrum of Muslim responses to such internal and external dynamics has been complex and varied. However, two mutually-exclusive broad patterns of response may, nevertheless, be discerned: a strong *reactionary traditionalist* perspective and an equally categorical *secularist-modernist* position. While the first tendency reduces Islam and the plurality of its historical expression to a monolithic ideology, constructed in opposition to what is perceived to be an invading and engulfing enemy, the latter attempts to make sense of Islam solely within the horizon of a particular Western apprehension of religion as confined to the private lives of individuals. Above all, our current context of Islam–West conflict has itself been a serious factor behind the emergence of such bipolar oppositions and uni-dimensional mind-sets.

Both of these perspectives have largely failed to develop a rigorous *dialectical engagement* with the profound processes of change facing the worldwide Muslim community (*umma*). Any meaningful engagement with the challenges posed by change depends upon the intellectual competence to revisit core Muslim values confidently in the light of ever-changing life conditions. An important factor behind the original historical rise of Muslim civilisation can be attributed to the deliberate nurture of such a competence for engagement within the overall framework of core Muslim values. This encouraged the early Muslims to value independent inquiry and to adopt a critically open attitude. *Ijtihad*, or independent reasoning, is the main intellectual concept that embodies these values and that refers to the dynamic and reflective process informing righteous conduct in all aspects of life. As such, the philosophy, science and wisdom of the ancient world – be it from Persia, India or Greece – was diligently collected, carefully studied and creatively re-interpreted by medieval Muslim scholarship. Their overall guiding principle was the central teaching of Islam – *tawhid*, literally the Oneness of God – which also supported the principle of the unity and interconnectedness of humanity, and thus of human knowledge, despite the vast cultural diversity from Spain to China to which they were exposed.

Such broad values of open enquiry and curiosity provided fertile conditions for the creative crosspollination of ideas and cultures to take place. As such, the development of distinctive Islamic approaches to administration, governance and culture was being constantly reinterpreted and negotiated. Thus, this early Islamization, contrary to some contemporary misconceptions, was a demotic and synthetic process that accommodated diversity, expressed within a unifying Islamic framework of meaning that received wide assent outside of mere creedal affiliation. In short, this Islamization supported a polyglot civilization not a monolithic faith. It may be admitted that qualities such as critical openness, independent inquiry and the accommodation of difference may sound distinctly modern to our ears and are sometimes depicted as achievements exclusive to Western secular democracy. Indeed, for some contemporary observers, like Mohammed Arkoun (2002), such qualities remain amongst what is 'unthought' in contemporary Islamic thinking. However, it may be observed that Arkoun's overall position reflects the above-mentioned categorical *secularist-modernist* perspective by which the Islamic worldview is taken to be a medieval relic that survives abnormally in the modern world, providing ample material for various deconstructionist experiments. However, these qualities are, above all, an important part of the human condition that are potentially available to any given society either to nurture or suppress. In its formative period, Islam, by endorsing openness, enquiry and tolerance, produced a just and balanced society that allowed people of different cultures, races and faiths to integrate into the Muslim commonweal while preserving their own dignity and ways of life.

However, once this *culture of engagement* was no longer nurtured, the result was a dramatic decline in the civilizational forces within Muslim polities. And it should be pointed out that the reification of dynamic core Muslim values into monolithic and authoritarian structures of power emerged long before the encounter with Western colonialism and secular modernity.

It is true that Muslims have been subjected to large-scale foreign invasions in the past such as the sacking of the Muslim powerhouse of intellectual engagement – Abbasid Baghdad – by the Mongols in 1258, which was significant also in putting an end to the first long-lasting and unified polity in the eastern Muslim world. Internally, the increasing sectarian strife and the spread of mystical views of Gnostic bent had begun to obscure core Muslim teachings. However, none of these challenges proved to be decisive enough to create a break with the values of cultural engagement. Thus, even under these deteriorating conditions, Muslim culture could still produce creative minds like al-Ghazali (d.1111) and Ibn Taymiyya (d.1328) that engaged critically with the inherited tradition and came up with meaningful Islamic responses to the challenges facing their societies. It is revealing too that they were more concerned with the decline in the Muslim culture of engagement than with the external military threats to Muslim rule. Ibn Taymiyya (1991, 1993, 1997), who called for tolerance and acceptance of diverse interpretations concerning the application of *shari'a*, argued forcefully that only through the adoption of a critical methodology could one judge the trustworthiness of inherited tradition and the soundness of reasoned argument. He was convinced that only a radical hermeneutics – discussed in greater detail below –

would reveal that reason and revelation were complementary and, most importantly, would ensure ways of discerning values and principles from the core Islamic sources and its diverse traditions under conditions of dramatic change so that each generation of Muslims might continue to be guided by them. As such Ibn Taymiyya demonstrated that Muslim culture, in its post-formative period, could still be creative in nurturing minds capable of exercising *ijtihad*.

Yet, during the period of rapid colonial and post-colonial modernisation, the voices for critical openness could not prevent a deep rupture within the modern Muslim psyche: linguistic, cultural and intellectual bridges of continuity with the cumulative Muslim tradition were not adequately maintained. Social theorists would argue too that, even under comparatively less stressful conditions, modernisation created a similar rupture in Europe with the religiously-based medieval Western tradition. However, even so, the Judeo-Christian tradition still contributed substantially to this long historical process of self-differentiation and social and institutional transformation that occurred in Western Europe. Today Muslims are still in the process of making sense of the imported ideas of modernity and its superimposed institutions upon Muslim polities. While the impulse for renewal and reform has not vanished, critical openness hardly thrives today. Rather the challenge of the West in the last two centuries has largely allowed the *reactionary traditionalist* Muslim trend to predominate. It advocates a retreat into the comforts of a glorious reified past instead of reconnecting with the culture of engagement so that Muslims may face their problems with realism. The phenomenon of *double alienation* has emerged: Muslims no longer feel comfortable within their own traditional cultures nor have they as yet integrated their core values with the best of what modernity, Western or otherwise, has to offer (Shayegan 1992).

Islam and Western secular democracy: dialogue or confrontation?

Despite strong contextual differences with their co-religionists in the Muslim world, the Muslim settlers in post-war Europe were not divorced from the unfolding narrative described previously. Besides being multi-ethnic and multilingual and often having strong rural roots in the Muslim world, the biggest factor for the European diaspora was its minority status, living in the midst of highly-secularised, multicultural societies. Some have full citizenship but even so are also often subject to socio-economic inequalities, discrimination and political suspicion, particularly after 9/11. While Western secular democratic states are undeniably more just and free than the more authoritarian political status quo in the Muslim world, a robust Islamic culture of engagement is, as yet, largely absent in the diaspora. This relatively low level of intellectual engagement has clearly influenced the way Muslim communities have publicly position-ed themselves within secular multicultural politics and the way the secular state perceives the personal and collective identities that Muslims express. My own empirical research (Sahin 2005) carried out among British Muslim youth found that they are intensely affected by the phenomenon of *double alienation*, which has led to what I would describe as an increasingly widespread foreclosed and depersonalised Muslim religiosity which can hardly facilitate positive faith development or provide them with the confidence to communicate effectively with the religious and cultural plurality around them.

In 2010 there are an estimated 17 million Muslims across Western Europe. Researchers and policymakers working within the dominant paradigm of integration (often imprecisely defined so as to be conflated with assimilation) focused on ethnic, linguistic and socio-economic structures underpinning these communities' interaction with the wider society. The emergence of faith as a central element underpinning new self-understanding was less recognised; the second and third generations often sought to negotiate their sense of identity in this new context by a return to religion.

Realising that they should abandon 'the myth of return', first-generation parents instead embraced 'the myth of continuity', creating narratives and institutions that would connect their children seamlessly with the religio-cultural mores of their own homeland upbringing. Transnational Islamic movements were often the first to seize upon this opportunity by providing the mosques and the imams to cater for this continuity. Thus, the British context has been largely disregarded in shaping the religious identity of the next generation and in conditioning their interaction within wider multicultural society.

Yet neither the Muslim communities nor policymakers have sufficiently prioritised the facilitation of a culture of engagement – particularly in the form of a long-term investment in education – to address both mainstreaming and radicalisation, empowering Muslim communities to identify ways of resolving their own problems. Instead, rather more short-term pragmatism seems to have prevailed in guiding the state's strategies to prevent extremism, given the focus on promoting 'moderate' Muslims or attempting to define British Muslim subjectivity through political rhetoric.

Without possessing the skills necessary for sustained cultural engagement, it is hard to see how Muslims will take on the challenges facing them effectively. Cultivating a mature Muslim presence in Europe requires the development and articulation of a comprehensive rationale for Islamic values and tradition in this context. The younger generation of Muslims is acutely aware and desirous of this shift towards a fully-fledged Muslim cultural engagement, a shift that requires the hermeneutical tools to interpret and understand core Islamic teachings and the cumulative tradition in the hope of producing meaningful Muslim responses.

Secularity as inclusion verses ideological secularism

Islam and the secular state has been subject of much discussion, which has largely been framed within the context of modern Muslim nation-states. Broadly speaking, for the *reactionary traditionalist* perspective, secularism represents an integral part of colonial modernisation as well as the promotion of atheism, denying any place for God's authority to be expressed within the social, political, juristic and economic spheres of modern society. Furthermore, secular culture is more or less equated with moral decadence and laxity, and, being characterised as such, it is deemed to be completely incompatible with Islam and its socio-political values. On the other hand, for the *secularist-modernist* perspective, Western secular modernity symbolises the ideal endpoint for national progress that Muslim culture should aspire to, or, even more sweepingly, that the Islamic tradition should be refashioned completely within its value framework. Intellectuals from those parts of the Muslim world that implemented the stricter French interpretation of secularism (or *laïcité* as the state promotion of anti-clericalism rather than as state neutrality with respect to religion) have argued that not only should Islam be kept away from politics but also from all aspects of the public sphere, e.g. the barring of religious dress at Turkish universities for instance. Furthermore, they have no interest in considering the place of faith within the social fabric and overall culture of the country. Instead, any attempt to bring religious values into any part of the public sphere is seen as a political challenge to the secular order and is portrayed as a 'theocratic Islamist threat'.

It is important for Muslims to acknowledge Europe's history of religious conflict, for that is the basis upon which we may appreciate how secularity signifies the emergence of the principle of reasoned politics that could potentially include and accommodate a grander diversity of cultures and values than was originally imagined at secularity's outset. The experiences of long inter-religious war and the authoritarian exercise of power by the Church hierarchy were countered by the humanist value of tolerance and the greater institutional separation between religion and state in the exercise of political and legal powers.

With this history in mind, the emergence of secularity need not necessarily be thought of as a rejection of religion altogether. To the contrary, some of the Enlightenment philosophers were religious in outlook and Christian ethical values still deeply informed European society of the day. It is arguable that the European Enlightenment need not be construed as the triumph of secular ideology over religion, but rather that of true religion over superstition, whose reformers dreamt of a spiritual republic based on moral foundations. In fact, the dramatic erosion of explicit Christian values might be dated much later to the post-1945 economic recovery and a new culture of consumption that led to a much wider social secularisation (Brown 2000). Moreover, I would argue that secularity, as a political process, has been interpreted and applied differently across Europe, with the differences between France's *laïcité* and Britain's moderate secularity (noted in greater detail in Chapter 5 by Tariq Modood than I can go into here). First of all there is the formal constitutional space for public religion that Anglican establishment offers. Secondly, minority faith groups have been granted recognition in the state school sector within the framework of substantial and historic faith school provision by the Christian church, as well as the equally important provision of multi-faith religious education within the secular educational system. And thirdly, there is the accommodative recognition by English common law of minority customs and practices that are deemed not to be in conflict with individual human rights. Thus, the fluid and accommodative nature of British secularism retains the capacity to further the development of inclusive and mature policies towards religion in public life.

However, it is also true that secularism as an ideological construct that places scientific rationality at the heart of the humanistic endeavour and additionally insists that reason ought to supersede religion is also an important part of the Enlightenment legacy today; in fact, many of the great social theorists almost naturalised this supersession of faith by reason as an inevitable outcome of modernity itself. Yet, even in Europe today, arguably the most secular of continents, the confident presence of religious diversity has shifted the terms of debate more towards the persistence of religion amidst talk that Europe has itself reached a post-secular stage.

Ironically, it is more often than not the case that, in trying to accommodate new religious communities, the European secular state expects, tacitly or otherwise, that their pattern of institutionalisation, religious authority and mode of public interaction should conform to Christian antecedents (Birt 2006). Here the real limitations of contemporary approaches by the secular state to non-Christian faith communities, that now define an important part of Europe's cultural reality, need to be carefully examined. Obviously Islam, given what I have outlined above as well as the reality of the current post-9/11 crisis, presents special challenges to European secular democracies. Equally, it seems to me that diverse faith communities face the challenge of recognising their own limitations – not to see the world solely from their own vantage point but to recognise their fundamental interdependence and their common sense of belonging together as part of the greater whole of society. As a process, secularity therefore creates the political space in which diverse worldviews and values may not only live in parallel with each other, but may also recognise their interdependence. This public and therefore political space, informed by the values of justice, respect and tolerance, holds the clue to perpetuating an egalitarian and just social order. Without clear justification and endorsement of these values from within one's own faith tradition, genuine integration will struggle to materialise. The precondition of achieving this relies upon engaging in self-criticism and critical openness to the other, for only then can our faith values be re-inscribed in our particular time and circumstance. It is as much a matter of cultural competence as of moral urgency to transform prejudice and discrimination into genuine mutual respect. And the responsibility of ethical engagement applies as much to the reactionary partisans of religion as it does to aggressive secular humanists.

This ethical engagement requires, even demands, sensitivity. Meaningful dialogue must not entail reducing the other to one's own categories of understanding, which is a less straightforward task than is often assumed. For instance, it is surprising how often engagement with Muslims seeks patterns of familiarity in their forms of collective representation and negotiation that are somehow analogues with the Church or in models of Christian religious leadership. Genuine dialogue really demands that we seek to transcend our life-worlds in the hope of reaching out to each other such that our individual and collective identities will gradually be redefined while living in 'the face of each other' (Sahin 2010). And the secular state, it seems to me, can create a sense of solidarity and common purpose if it nurtures this cultural civility within the multiplicity of values and ways of life that together define its polity, a nurturing that is built upon the safeguarding of basic religious freedoms. On the other hand, a political culture that views the presence of public religion as inherently malignant cannot, I would argue, foster a genuine culture of dialogue, critical openness and engagement.

Are Muslim social and political values necessarily in conflict with secular democratic culture?

It is often argued that Islam, from its inception and throughout most of its history, has been a faith of empire, and that diversity was tolerated, even encouraged, but only within the context of Muslim political predominance. Moreover, Islam developed a strong political theology that theorised a state structure intolerant of internal dissent and defined external relations by reference to continuous war between Islam and unbelief. Thus, it is concluded that unless Islam is thoroughly secularised, and drops its claim to the public sphere, it will remain incompatible with the requirements of modern life. With respect to Islam as a minority faith within an overarching secular Western context, its prosperity is predicated upon working contentedly within the public and private spaces defined by the secular state.

These are important concerns that should not be brushed aside. However, at the same time, there is naïve logic at work behind them if we are concerned to develop an Islamic perspective within the radically different circumstances of Muslim communities living within Britain's secular multicultural society. We need, I would suggest, in interpreting our tradition in the face of contemporary challenges to be guided by a radical hermeneutics – identified by scholars like Ibn Taymiyya (more normally enlisted, I would argue erroneously, in the name of the *reactionary traditionalist* trend) – as lying at the heart of the Islamic intellectual vocation.

A central part of this hermeneutic strategy is to consider seriously: (i) the character of Muslim faith; (ii) the nature of its core sources, the Qur'an and the Prophetic tradition; and (iii) the overall values that have guided the development of the early Muslim community under prophetic leadership and thereafter.

First of all, there is matter of how faith in Islam should be characterised: is it a matter of mere submission or of being *critically* faithful? The Qur'anic terms for 'faith' are the Arabic verbal nouns of *islam* and *iman*, both of which describe an existential mode, or a distinct way of being human, rather than indicating subscription to or belief in cognitive content. The closest Qur'anic analogue to a belief system is the word *i'tiqad*, meaning tying, binding or committing oneself to a certain core value, and thus the term also has strong existential implications. According to the Qur'anic worldview, since God is the Creator of all life and has endowed humanity with the capacity for intelligence and the task of stewardship of the earth (*khalifa*) (2:30, 7:74), He deserves recognition for this. Thus being faithful (*muslim* or *mu'min*) entails the voluntary human act of acknowledging God's favours upon humanity through the recognition that He alone is worthy of worship and adoration (*'ibadat*). In return, the Qur'an stresses that God remains 'grateful (*shakir*) for whosoever does good voluntarily by rewarding their good conduct bountifully' (2:158). Therefore, just as the Qur'an links faithfulness with thankfulness, another existential state, rejection (*kufr*) is tied together with ingratitude, or a failure to acknowledge God's favours. The Qur'an develops a distinct educational theory and embodies a Divine pedagogy that seeks to bring humanity to a state of faithfulness and gratitude. Revelation plays the role of aiding human reasoning to discern meaning whilst reflecting on creation as a whole. Indeed, the Qur'an does not deny the reality of scepticism but sees such questioning as integral to human reasoning. While retelling the story of Abraham's discovery of monotheism, the Qur'an acknowledges scepticism as a necessary part of a healthy growth into faith (2:260, 6:75-80).

The critical voice is most vividly illustrated in the Qur'an too when it comes to opposing injustice and oppression within society. When given proper attention, the critical voice embedded within the Qur'an's highly rhetorical language becomes clearer. For instance, the critique of Christology or the reification of divine law within Judaism are central to the Qur'an's critical engagement with what constitutes extremism and moderation in religion itself (2:143, 3:79, 4:171, 5:77). The faithful community is itself, therefore, not immune from the Qur'an's critical gaze as it is constantly invited to repent and warned that if it deviates from the truth and from righteous conduct it should be aware that God's mercy is not the exclusive property of any community, particularly of those who would always seek to claim, for political reasons, that they are on the side of truth and justice without subjecting themselves to critical self-reflection and examination (2:105, 3:73-74).

As an existential category, living a life of gratitude involves a strong social dimension, and thus Muslims are encouraged to work towards a faithful politics that is just and balanced.

Therefore, the values of societal dealings and personal conduct and character (*mu'amalat, adab, akhlaq*) alongside a commitment to the values of faith (*i'tiqad*) and worship (*'ibadat*) are part and parcel of Muslim religiosity. The concept of *shari'a* signifies the application of Islamic values to create and safeguard a faithful society, while the broader Islamic concept of *tawhid*, or the Oneness of God, underscores the interconnected nature of human life. The Qur'an is realistic about the contextual character of the human condition, clearly recognising that core divine values may only ever be practised within a particular historical and cultural context: for each society there is an assigned law and way of life (*shir'atan wa minhaja*) (5:48, 45:18); each society has its own appointed time (10:49); each has its own appointed book (13:38); and it is only God Who is the ultimate source of all revelation (13:39).

The Qur'an contains not only this broad value framework defining the character of being faithful but also proposes hermeneutic strategies that guide the process of producing the faithful personality, a faithful politics and developing Islamically-meaningful responses to the ever-changing practicalities of life. The emergence of the first historical Muslim community under prophetic leadership illustrates the concrete application of these principles in bringing about a just and balanced society. These principles constitute the foundations of Muslim imagination in interpreting the world, which are, in turn, firmly grounded in the deeper ethical relationship of trust between God and humanity. It should be stressed that the more specialized exegetical methodologies, which flourished among the diverse genres of classical Muslim scholarship, including legal theory, are necessarily limited expressions, rooted in the more fundamental production of meaning defined by the Qur'anic horizon. There is not the space here to discuss in greater detail this broader interpretive framework or to consider further its implications for engaging with the challenges facing modern Muslim societies. However, attempts at methodological reconstruction within the classical Islamic disciplines and particularly in Islamic law need to reconnect and re-root themselves in the deeper interpretative dynamism offered by the Qur'anic worldview (al-Jabri 2009). This would help to go beyond the narrow confines of explaining and interpreting the texts without due regard for the world around us, in order to allow the interpretive act (*tafsir, ta'wil*) to produce Islamically-meaningful responses to our current context.

The Qur'an illustrates that God *reasons* with humanity in communicating the Divine message, providing justifications for its call alongside a marked attention to the human condition and its intricate challenges. Humanity is, above all, entrusted with the task of engaging in an open and honest dialogical process (*shura*) to arrive at working and meaningful consensus (*ijma'*) in managing justly their life affairs (2:233, 3:159, 39:18). The Qur'an particularly on social issues such as public security that concerns the wellbeing of all explicitly demands the exercise of evidence-based reasoning and interpretations to guide the community (4:83).Therefore, the human capacity to comprehend and argue for just and reasonable conduct and thereafter to turn this into legitimate and socially-accepted cultural practices and customs (*'urf* and *ma'ruf*) is acknowledged and seen as complementing the Divine revelation (2:233, 7:199). Moreover, the Qur'an embraces the ethnic, linguistic, cultural and religious diversity of human life and insists that this irreducible difference should not be the cause of suspicion or discrimination but should instead provide a powerful motive for 'knowing one another' (49:13) and for competing to advance human welfare and goodness (5:48).

The Qur'anic perception of being faithful requires constant and critical vigilance (*muhasaba*) upon the individual and social aspects of life, which has, as mentioned above, among its essential features the encouragement of good conduct in the widest possible sense through 'commanding good and forbidding wrong' (*amr bi'l-ma'ruf wa nahy 'an al-munkar*). Classical Muslim legal thought, in reflecting upon on social and political issues in the light of this fundamental Qur'anic principle, was not only concerned with the practicalities of 'forbidding wrong' but also deliberated upon the implications of the fact that God *reasons with* humanity while communicating His Divine message. The classic tradition also meditated upon the implications of revising legal rulings in the light of changing contexts, the importance of consultation (*shura*) and the centrality of public criticism.

Therefore it is unsurprising to see that Muslim scholars engaged with the task of discerning the fundamental causes, intents and principles of the Divine message (*istinbat 'ilal wa maqasid*), and centred that task around upholding inalienable human dignity (*karama*) (17:62/70) through the preservation of human life, property, family, freedom of thought and so forth. The Andalusian Maliki jurist Imam al-Shatibi (d.1388) is a well-known figure who by studying the 'legal intent' (*maqasid*) of the sacred scripture re-rooted the *shari'a* within these broad principles that preserve human dignity and welfare. Najm al-Din al-Tufi (d. 1316), a key figure in the Hanbali legal school, offered a more original perspective in re-connecting Islamic law with the radical social ethics embedded within core Muslim teachings. Al-Tufi, while reflecting upon the authentic prophetic report that '[There should be] no causing or being subjugated to harm', grounded Islamic legal theory within the concept of prompting the public good (*maslaha*). Al-Tufi's radicalism was to follow the logical consequences of the *maqasid* governing the Qur'anic world-view by foregrounding the scared text within the fundamental principle of the common good (*maslaha*), as for him the overall hermeneutic discernment of the text revealed one overarching *raison d'être* for the Divine Will – to preserve human dignity and the common interest of society. This replacement of effect for cause therefore allows for the more immediate application of core Islamic values in radically changed contexts. And it is noteworthy that while al-Tufi's argument has attracted criticism from some modern scholars, the views of his contemporary and teacher Ibn Taymiyya were not dissimilar.

Indeed, al-Tufi himself pre-empted some possible objec-
tions to and misunderstandings of his thinking. He was quick
to point out that the Divine regulations concerning worship, the
essential part of Muslim religiosity, were not part of his discussion. He also argued that while we may identify countless benefits
and wisdoms behind the prescribed acts of worship, it is difficult
to discern one overriding cause behind these obligations as they
exclusively belong to the category of *God's rights*. However, when
carefully considered, the Divine teachings and rules governing
the broad range of human social activity (*mu'amalat*), al-Tufi
insisted, ultimately aim to preserve the common good and social
welfare (*maslaha*). Nearly all the legal schools of thought recognise *maslaha* as an important source within Islamic law (*shari'a*),
but al-Tufi goes one step further in suggesting that *maslaha* is
indeed the central principle upon which the *shari'a* is built. As
such, he argues strongly that *maslaha* and textual principles and
rulings are complementary with each other; if a conflict arises
between the two then the principle of the common good and the
pursuit of social welfare should be given the primary attention.
He further defends his position – anticipating further objec-
tion – by drawing attention to the fact that, within classical legal
theory, the jurists had already classified textual pronouncements
as being general (*'amm*), particular (*khass*), abrogating (*naskh*)
and abrogated (*mansukh*), when considering their application to
a particular and given social context. Indeed, the jurists talked at
times of the Prophetic *Sunna* gaining primacy over the Qur'an by
virtue of its explanatory nature, providing detail to the general
Qur'anic injunctions. As such, al-Tufi argued for the need to
conjoin together these special features of the text and realities
of the social context while developing Islamic responses to the
challenge of new situations. Al-Tufi's efforts are clearly aimed at
what I pointed to earlier as the urgent need to re-connect the
dynamic Qur'anic world-view with changing social realities in
an Islamically-meaningful way. Of course both al-Tufi and Ibn
Taymiyya stressed that the common good should be interpreted

within the wider boundaries of Islamic values (*dawabit*), but, so long as these boundaries were not violated, Muslims could work conscientiously to uphold the common good in any society where they lived. Both knew well, for instance, that the Prophet Muhammad insisted that he would have continued, after his Prophetic calling, to take part in the committee set up in pre-Islamic Mecca to protect visiting traders.

As mentioned above, in theological terms, gratitude to God, in the form of worshiping Him alone, is recognised as having social and political manifestations. God's rightful command that the ethical and legal values of Islam are instituted is manifested through bringing about a faithful politics of justice and moderation (*ummatan wasatan*). This is depicted as taking place within the framework of human rights (*huquq al-'ibad*), and, as such, Islamic legal theory has developed a strong rights-based approach that grounds the rights and responsibilities of the legal subject (*mukallaf*) within the rule of law (Hallaq 2006).

In general terms, while political theology in Islam reflects the above-mentioned egalitarian ethical and social values, terming this 'theocracy' is the least accurate way to describe it. As Muhsin Mahdi (2001) points out, Islamic political theology sought to put an end to the ancient Middle Eastern notion of divine kingship. While it is true that the Prophet Muhammad combined both spiritual and political offices, he did *not* claim to have received Divine knowledge with respect to many worldly matters, which remained within the realm of human experience and reasoning. For instance, tradition records that some of his political decisions were challenged by his Companions, in other words, that the Prophet's decision-making was itself guided by the egalitarian message of the Qur'an. As such, while neither the Qur'an nor the Prophetic tradition has left us with a strictly-defined Islamic political system, they have both strongly charged the faithful with the task of upholding justice through preserving human dignity – in short, with the task of furthering a balanced socio-political order. Thus, within the Muslim polity, religion and politics are meant to be complementary as a necessary reflection of Islam's basic holistic attitude towards life and the undeniable diversity of human experience.

This complementary nature suggests that the core Muslim values should guide human activity in its personal articulations as well as complex social organisations including political governance. The main function of values remain pedagogic in essence in that they are assumed to be managing power relations in order to bring society towards an ideal maturity and moderation. At the same time these core values inform the boundaries of legality and acceptability to which both individuals and social organisations, including the state apparatus, need to confirm. Political governance is central in maintaining the security of the public but its legitimacy is conditioned with its capacity to distribute justice, and to safeguard the rights of God and those of the public alike. Thus, it is not surprising to observe that historically Muslim culture has placed a special emphasis on the concept of *legality*, or *shari'a*, the wider ethico-legal value framework that remains the key to legitimising civil and political activity. As discussed above, the historical reception and application of these values have not been monolithic but plural in character: even in strictly legal terms, multiple authorities in the form of diverse schools of thought have been firmly recognised. The role of learned specialists, the *'ulama'*, who authoritatively and independently discern and interpret this fundamental value framework for society, has always been crucial. However, it should be stressed that they are not beyond accountability. What qualifies this highly esteemed position of *'ulama'* is neither their charisma nor their membership of a particular family-clan or lineage but the depth of their understanding and observance of Islamic teachings and values. Thus, those *'ulama'* who possess an expert knowledge and understanding of Islam and its values are seen as the inheritors of the Prophetic legacy and role and are therefore charged with the responsibility of facilitating a critical engagement between civil society and political power to advance the cause of individual rights and the welfare of the society at large.

A re-consideration of the various genres of classical Islamic political theology – the legal rules of governance (*ahkam al-sultan-iyya*), or the more explicitly philosophical and ethical tracts – supports my contention. Asma Asfaruddin's exploration (2002) of the prolific *manaqib* literature (the virtues and excellence of the legitimate ruler) rightly argues that both the Sunni doctrine of the caliphate and the Shiite doctrine of the imamate originally centred on the need for ethical justification. Thus personal virtue or piety, rather than the simple fact of one's kingship, provided the necessary legitimacy for power, which is indeed in agreement with the Qur'anic message that the fortunes of a people or nation depend upon their merits and moral excellence (10:13-14). Similarly, in the classical Islamic tradition, the proper conduct of politics was bound by ethics and law: kings were not held to rule as of divine right. Today of course this means that the faithful Muslim is concerned not so much with the process and form of politics but with the relationship between politics and ethics. It is not secularity as such that is in question but whether it may deliver up the higher values to which politics itself ought to be committed.

It has not been my intent with this brief exposition of Islamic political theology to deal with all the detailed implications of living faithfully as a Muslim under a secular politics, but to ask the more fundamental question about the relationship between politics and faith. There are certainly many particular issues that need further deliberation from within the critically-faithful perspective that I have been arguing for. To sum up the concluding argument briefly, it has been my contention that Islam strongly encourages us Muslims – whether we live in a minority or majority context – to participate actively within democratic and secular politics to promote the common good and the welfare and dignity of all.

References

Abed al-Jabri, M. (2009) *Democracy, Human Rights and Law in Islamic Thought* (New York: I.B. Tauris)

Arkoun, M. (2002) *The Unthought in Contemporary Islamic Thought* (London: Saqi Books).

Asfaruddin, A. (2002) *Excellence and Precedence: Medieval Islamic Discourse on Legitimate Leadership* (Leiden: Brill).

Birt, J. (2006) 'Good Imam, Bad Imam: Civic Religion and National Integration in Britain post-9/11', *The Muslim World*, 96: 687-705.

Brown, C.G. (2000) *The Death of Christian Britain: Christianity and Society in the Modern World* (London: Routledge).

Hallaq, W.B. (2006) *The Origins and Evolution of Islamic Law* (Cambridge: University Press).

Ibn Taymiyya, Ahmad (1991) *Qa'ida fi Tawahhud al-Milla wa Ta'addud al-Shara'i, Majmu' al-Fatawa* 19: 9-65 (Riyadh: Dar 'alam al-kutub).

—— (1993) *Al-Siyasa al-Shai'iyya fi al-Islah wa al-Ra'iyyah* (Beirut: Dar Al-Jil).

—— (1997) *Dar' Ta'arud al-'Aql wa al-Naql* (Beirut: Dar al-Kutub al-'Ilmiyya).

Mahdi, M. (2001) *Alfarabi and the Foundation of Islamic Political Philosophy* (Chicago: University Press).

Negin, N. (2003) *Intellectuals and the State in Iran: Politics, Discourse, and the Dilemma of Authenticity* (Gainsville, FL.: University Press of Florida).

Shayegan, D. (1992) *Cultural Schizophrenia: Islamic Societies Confronting the West* (London: Saqi Books).

Sahin, A. (2005) 'Exploring the religious life-world and attitude toward Islam among British Muslim adolescents', in L. Francis *et al.* (eds.), *Religion and Adolescence: International Perspectives* (Cardiff: University of Wales Press), pp. 164-84.

Sahin, A. (2010) 'Authority and Autonomy: An Islamic Education Perspective on Human Agency' in Marcio Buitelaar *et al.* (eds.) *Islam and Autonomy: International Perspectives* (Leuven: Peeters), pp. 150-76.

Al-Tufi, Najm al-Din (1992) *Risala fi Ri'ayat al-Maslaha* (Beirut: Dar al-Kutub al-'Ilmiyya).

Chapter 2

~

The need for religious secularity

Nick Spencer

The second half of the twentieth century was dominated by a conflict between two irreconcilably opposed superpowers. Their values were fundamentally different and incompatible and each was, at least in theory, prepared to defend itself to the death.

This was the battle between capitalism and communism; between freedom and equality; between the small state and the totalitarian state; and for some, between godliness and godlessness. East was east and West was west and the two could not conceivably meet.

Except that, rather peculiarly, the US and the USSR were both *secular* states. This secularism blurred a little in the case of America during the first decade of the Cold War when, in 1954, Congress passed a bill that added the words 'under God' to the nation's Pledge of Allegiance, and then again two years later when President Eisenhower made 'In God We Trust' the national motto (Domke and Coe 2008).

But in spite of such concessions made to a nervous nation, the fact remains that Article 6 of the US Constitution ('No religious Test shall ever be required as a Qualification to any Office or public Trust under the United States') and the first amendment ('Congress shall make no law respecting an establishment of religion, or prohibiting the free exercise thereof') stood (and stand) as distinctive cornerstones of US politics. Indeed, so distinctive are they that, according to a recent study of the relations between state and religion in 175 countries, 'at the federal level, the USA is unique among all countries ... in that it has absolute SRAS [Separation of Religion and State]' (Fox 2008).

As to the USSR, you don't have to go too far to find its secular roots. Shortly after the Revolution of 1917, the innocuous sounding and impeccably secular 'Decree on the Freedom of Conscience and on Church and Religious Associations' was passed, separating the Orthodox Church from the state, and appearing to guarantee freedom of both religion and irreligion. The reality was, of course, very different, with the Orthodox Church and others being deprived of their legal personalities, having lands and properties nationalised, and with 'crimes' such as giving religious instruction or 'inspiring superstition in the masses' meriting up to a year's 'corrective labour' (Burleigh 2006).

The formation of The Soviet League of the Militant Godless in 1925 helped to centralise and cement these efforts, in the process using slogans that have a bizarrely modern ring to them: 'Science instead of religion'; 'Destroying religion, we say: study science'; 'Religion is poison: protect your children'; 'Terrorists in Cassocks'; 'We want to sweep away everything that claims to be supernatural...'; 'Without God, our affairs are much better' (Peris 1998).

The manner in which both the US and the USSR can legitimately lay claim to being secular warns us of the elasticity of the term. Even within the infinitely more measured and careful world of academic reflection, there is considerable disagreement over its precise meaning, with Charles Taylor beginning his recent magnum opus, *A Secular Age*, by outlining three distinct modes of understanding it (Taylor 2007).[1]

With an eye to the question of what *theological* grounds there are for the category of the secular within contemporary Islamic, Jewish and Christian thought, I want to argue that the kind of aggressive secularism that was practised in the USSR (and is still preached in some quarters today) is by no means the only necessary form and that, properly understood, secularism is not only compatible with religious faith, but is rather a legitimate and necessary means of expressing that faith.

The origins of the secular

The word secular is first found in English in the late thirteenth century and derives from the Latin word *sæculum*, meaning 'age', 'span of time' or 'generation'. The concept found a rich seam in the twin-track Christianity of the late Middle Ages, but, as we shall see, it is in fact as old as Christianity itself.

The early Christians believed that the resurrection of Christ inaugurated a new age – they were the original New Agers. It was a time in which God, through his crucified, resurrected and ascended messiah had made good on his promises of liberation and redemption, freeing his terminally-rebellious creatures from their sin and its effects.

Followers of Christ were charged with living under this new regime and telling the world about it. But this caused problems. The gospel, as it came to be known, was politically subversive. Indeed, even the word *evangelion*, from which we get 'gospel', whilst having roots in the Old Testament, was an adaptation of the annunciation of imperial good news, such as a birth, accession, military achievement, or establishment of *Pax Romana*.

---

[1] They are (a) 'public spaces...[that] have been allegedly emptied of God'; (b) 'falling off of religious belief or practice'; (c) the condition of society in which 'belief in God ... is understood to be one option among others, and frequently not the easiest to embrace.' Taylor chooses to examine the third option.

According to Christians, Jesus Christ was the world's Lord, not Caesar: he offered 'peace and security' (an imperial idiom), not Caesar; and he now ruled by means of the cross, not Caesar. Christians' citizenship and loyalty lay, first and foremost, with the risen Christ, not the earthly emperor.

And yet Christianity was not a politically revolutionary movement in the sense we understand that term. Christians were not interested in overthrowing the public authorities, but merely in putting them in their place. The authorities still had a critical role to play, depending on your theology, in maintaining public order, providing social infrastructure and/or securing the common good.

Crucially, however, that role did not entail accreting to themselves the power and authority of the divine. Christians were mandated to respect the authorities but not to worship them. In the words of one early Christian, 'I will pay honour to the emperor not by worshipping him but by praying for him.' (O'Donovan and O'Donovan 1999)

This resulted in an ongoing, low-level tension between the public authorities and this troublesome but growing sect, which occasionally erupted into bouts of grotesque persecution. In this way, the emergence of Christianity – with its combination of continued respect for and loyalty towards public authority in the midst of a proclamation of a new age, all founded on Christ – lay the foundation for what we now know as the secular, a public space in which authorities should be respected but can be legitimately challenged and may never accord to themselves absolute or ultimate significance (Spencer 2006).

From these origins it may readily be seen how the 'secular' came, ultimately in some quarters, to stand foursquare against the Christian, indeed against the religious believer in general. When the word first appeared in Middle English, it was used to mean 'worldly' or, more precisely, 'belonging to this world or age'. The term was used in respect of 'secular clergy', who lived with their flock, as opposed to 'religious' or 'spiritual' clergy who lived away from the distractions of this world, usually within a monastic order.

A few hundred years later, when the word 'secularisation' was first coined, it was used to mean 'the conversion of an ecclesiastical or religious institution or its property to civil possession and use' or 'the conversion of an ecclesiastical state or sovereignty to a lay one'.

It is a short step from such usages to the word coming to stand for something that is intentionally non- or anti-religious. This is precisely how it came to be used, by Christians and atheists alike, in nineteenth-century England, when one of the most prominent anti-religious figures of the Victorian period, George Holyoake, first used the word 'secularism' to mean the 'doctrine that morality should be based on the well-being of man in the present life, without regard to religious belief or a hereafter.'

Interestingly, the double meaning remained even as 'secularism', in its anti-religious sense, grew. Holyoake and Charles Bradlaugh, Britain's first openly atheist Member of Parliament, clashed over whether they should use the term 'secularist' or 'atheist', Holyoake preferring the former because, he insisted, it did not necessitate the latter (Berman 1998). It is by means of this long, winding and diverging etymological stream that we came to the absurdity of both the USSR and USA laying claim to the mantle of secularism in the twentieth century, and the reason why people in Britain today, not least religious ones, are so confused by the term.

Disentangling the secular

The first step, then, is to disentangle the two kinds of secularism. It is this disentangling that is in evidence in Abdullah Sahin's separation of *secularity* and *secularism* in Chapter 1. The secular state, in the former sense, is one in which we 'can create a sense of solidarity and common purpose ... [nurturing] cultural civility within the multiplicity of values and ways of life.' This is something that all religious believers should welcome and work towards.

The secular state, in the latter sense of 'secularism' constitutes 'a political culture that views the presence of public religion as inherently malignant [and] cannot ... foster a genuine culture of dialogue, critical openness and engagement.' This, it hardly needs stating, is not appealing to religious believers.

This is similar to the distinction that the Archbishop of Canterbury, Rowan Williams, has made between 'programmatic' secularism and 'procedural' secularism (Williams 2006). Williams' 'programmatic secularism' is 'secularism' as Sahin has termed it, the 'Soviet-style' approach (which is readily found, in attenuated forms, among British broadsheet commentators today) in which religion is compulsorily privatised, for all sorts of spurious reasons relating to reasonableness, liberty and social cohesion. Conversely, Williams' 'procedural secularism' is Sahin's 'secularity', or, in Williams' words, 'a crowded and argumentative public square which acknowledges the authority of a legal mediator or broker whose job it is to balance and manage real difference.' This is secularism as an attempt to deal fairly with all religious and irreligious commitments, or American rather than Soviet-style secularism. It is, in effect, a modern, worked-through version of the kind of understanding of the secular that emerged, in embryonic form, in the early Christian centuries.

Abdullah Sahin's analysis and approval of 'secularity' is, I believe, encouraging not only because it resonates with my own convictions but because active religious engagement with secularity is positively necessary.[2] That is not simply so that we can then all live together in some warm, cuddly, secular utopia, but rather because when we arrive at one point of consensus –

---

[2] For the sake of continuity and clarity I shall stick to Sahin's terms of 'secularity' and 'secularism' for the remainder of this chapter, although I think they might be easily exchanged for 'procedural' and 'programmatic' secularism respectively – and I dare say other terms besides.

i.e. that 'secularity' is, by and large, a good thing for us all – we cannot settle there.

This is partly because some would-be advocates of 'secularity', who loudly espouse the 'equal playing field' rationale, frequently slip into 'secularism' by attempting to exclude from effective public debate those motivated by a comprehensive *religious* doctrine for a whole variety of questionable reasons. One only has to read comments on debate over gay adoption or stem-cell research to see that.

But there is also a more positive reason for Muslims and others to engage positively with 'secularity'. It is that 'secularity' is anything but a done deal. Agreeing to abide by the rules of 'secularity' leaves everyone, religious groups included, with two tasks: firstly, to design and modify those rules and, second, to engage in debate within them. I would like to explore these two tasks, dealing roughly with the *process* and the *content* of policy, separately, using a legendarily controversial example to illustrate my point.

Secularity and the process of policy

Abortion law varies from one country to another, as do the means of deciding those laws. In Britain, it is decided by Members of Parliament (MPs) who periodically vote, by convention on a free vote, on whether to amend the 1967 Abortion Act.

In the US, by contrast, the matter is decided by the Supreme Court, which ruled in *Roe v. Wade* (1973) that all state and federal laws outlawing or restricting abortion violated a constitutional right to privacy under the Due Process Clause of the Fourteenth Amendment.

The difference between these two modes of decision-making is significant and has been cited as the reason why abortion in the US is such an all-encompassing, make-or-break, near-hysterical subject whereas in the UK it is merely an emotive and controversial one.

Whether one realises it or not such modes of decision-making are formed by conceptions of the good, which are themselves formed by our own religious or other commitments. In the US, a decision that resulted in the termination of millions of pregnancies was made by nine people, none of whom were democratic representatives, and was justified by the sixth clause of an amendment that was originally proposed in 1866 to secure the rights of former slaves. Not surprisingly, opponents of the decision have objected that it lacks a valid constitutional foundation, and have tried to argue that the issue should be decided by the democratic process and state legislatures, as it was before the Roe case.

In the UK, by contrast, the decision is made by democratic means with MPs being given a free vote by convention because abortion, like other issues relating to the start of life, is deemed to be such a strongly-held 'moral' issue that parties will not make a manifesto commitment about it. Accordingly, this special 'freedom of conscience' clause irritates some who claim, and I would argue rightly so, that *all* political issues are moral issues.

The point here is not to outline what is the right way for determining such an issue, still less to decide what abortion law there should be. Rather it is to show that, even within a system of 'secularity' – in which everyone agrees that the ultimate decision should be political rather than, say, ecclesiastical, debated rather than asserted, and respected rather than violated – there is still scope for debating *how* we establish the process of arriving at that decision. Should such an issue be decided by democratic representatives? Should it be decided at a state or federal level? Should representatives be entitled to vote with their conscience in such matters but not in others? If so, should that right be secured by legislation or merely be a matter of convention? Should a constitution, or an amendment thereto, legitimately be used to pronounce on an issue like abortion, not least if the amendment itself does not directly refer to the issue? What are the merits of a written constitution in the first place?

Each of these is a substantive issue, which can only be adjudicated by drawing on substantive conceptions of the good. All such conceptions, whether rooted in a religious worldview or not, need to be heard in such debates. If not, a portion of society is worryingly disenfranchised. In the words of the political scientist Jonathan Chaplin,

> Where society is pervasively secularised – where public life and institutions are principally governed as if transcendent religious authority is irrelevant – it will in practice almost inevitably lean towards programmatic secularism [i.e. Sahin's secularism]. (Chaplin 2009)

Secularity and the content of policy

Much the same can be said regarding the second task facing those who engage positively with secularity, i.e. engaging in the debate that takes place within the agreed rules. Staying with our example, the *Roe v. Wade* decision passed by the Supreme Court in 1973 judged that a mother may abort her pregnancy for any reason, up until the 'point at which the foetus becomes "viable"', with the court defining viable as being 'potentially able to live outside the mother's womb, albeit with artificial aid.' In 2008, when abortion last came before the UK Parliament, MPs voted to keep the limit at 24 weeks for a similar reason.

It hardly needs saying that these positions are based on very substantive conceptions of the good. Each position one adopts on abortion – whether (i) never, (ii) only in cases of severe foetal abnormality, (iii) during the first, second or third trimester, (iv) at week 20, 22 or 24, (v) on demand or not, (vi) with the consent of two doctors or fewer, and so on – depends very heavily on the relative weight one places on the values of human life, dependence, autonomy and choice.

The idea that it is legitimate to permit abortion up till the point at which a foetus becomes viable is based on a *belief* of what makes a human life valuable, in this instance relating to its capacity for independence and autonomy. Given *that* particular belief, *that* position on abortion is 'rational'. But given foundations that are formed by different conceptions of the good, other conclusions are equally 'rational'.

It was perfectly 'rational' for ancient Romans to expose (i.e. leave to die on the street) unwanted infants, especially girls, given the value they assigned to human life, especially female life. It is perfectly 'rational' for modern Catholics to campaign for an end to all abortion given the way they understand human life. It is a myth, pure and simple – indeed, worse, it is a confidence trick – to claim that one position is more 'rational' than any other *simpliciter*. A position may be more or less rational given its particular premises, but all positions, all public doctrines, are based on an element of 'faith'.

This, incidentally, is one of the reasons why religious people refer to humanism and similar ideologies as 'faiths'. It is not simply to irritate humanists, although I have noticed it tends to do that, but rather to point out that if you want to say anything serious and consequential about a public issue, and humanists undoubtedly do, you need at some point to assume premises, a worldview if you like, that are based on foundations or values that you cannot prove.

The point of this discussion, once again, is not to adjudicate on the content of abortion law, any more than the previous one was to judge the process of arriving at that law. Rather, it is to repeat that there are still real issues that are up for grabs, even if we all operate in a 'secular' system under which such decisions are debated in the public square and decision-making is then respected by the public. It is vital that religious people participate in such debates. Without religious voices, public debate would be tidier, of course, but much impoverished – and done at the expense of excluding valid views and, crucially, of disenfranchising those believers who hold them.

In conclusion, if we all agreed on the legitimacy of 'secularity', it would certainly be a start. But it wouldn't be an end.

'Secularity' can be coloured by different ideologies, as readily as any other public doctrine. What we need, to stand alongside and engage with the liberal 'secularity' that is such a clear and powerful voice in our society, is an informed and respectful *religious* 'secularity', be it Christian, Jewish or Muslim or any other religious group. The term may sound as oxymoronic as 'secular clergy' does to us today, but it is no less valid or needed for it.

References

Berman, D. (1988) *A history of atheism in Britain* (London: Routledge).

Burleigh, M. (2006) *Earthly Powers: Religion and Politics from the European Dictators to Al Qaeda* (London: Harper Press).

Chaplin, J. (2009) *Talking God: The legitimacy of religious public reasoning* (London: Theos).

Domke, D., and K. Coe (2008) *The God Strategy: How Religion Became a Political Weapon in America* (Oxford: University Press).

Fox, J. (2008) *A World Survey of Religion and the State* (Cambridge: University Press).

O'Donovan, O., and J.L. O'Donovan (1999) *From Irenaeus to Grotius: A Sourcebook in Christian Political Thought* (Cambridge: Eerdmans).

Peris, D. (1998) *Storming the Heavens: The Soviet League of the Militant Godless* (Ithaca, NY: Cornell University Press).

Taylor, C. (2007) *A Secular Age* (Cambridge, MA: Belknap Press).

Spencer, N. (2006) *'Doing God': A future for faith in the public square* (London: Theos).

Williams, R. (2006) 'Secularism, Faith and Freedom', lecture delivered at the Pontifical Academy of Social Sciences, Rome, 23 November, available at http://www.archbishopofcanterbury.org/654, accessed 21 April 2009.

Chapter 3

~

Secularity and Religious Values

Norman Solomon

I warmly welcome Abdullah Sahin's clear analysis of difficulties facing Muslims within the new global order dominated by Western liberal culture, and strongly endorse his call for dialogue rather than confrontation. Frequently, as he was speaking, I felt that I could substitute 'Jew' for 'Muslim', 'Jewish' for 'Islamic', Yehuda haLevi (d. 1142) for al-Ghazali (d. 1111) and so on, without compromising the discourse, so close have our experiences been.

In my response to Abdullah Sahin's paper, however, I shall focus on areas where I feel there is room for further discussion rather on those in which we find ourselves in complete agreement.

Secularity and Secularism

Abdullah Sahin distinguishes between secularity and secularism. Secularity, by which he understands the impartiality of government with regard to the religious faith of its citizens, a notion akin to Charles Taylor's 'programmatic secularism', may be compatible with Islamic values; on the other hand secularism, 'an ideological position that confines faith strictly to the personal sphere of life', is, he maintains, inherently incompatible with Islam.

Let us consider in more detail exactly what is meant when we describe Britain as a 'secular state'. By this term I understand, as does Abdullah Sahin, a state whose *administration* is impartial as to the religious faith of its citizens; that is, its laws apply without discrimination to people of all religions, and no privileges are granted or withheld on the grounds of religion. (A state ought not to discriminate on grounds of colour, race or gender either, but that is nothing to do with being secular.)

On this definition Britain is not quite a secular state. It has – as Abdullah Sahin noted – an established church; some of the officials of this church (the monarch, some bishops) are *ex officio* part of the legislature. The Church of England, moreover, is assumed as the default religious affiliation of citizens, at least in England; its cathedrals and churches dominate the landscape, its festivals (Christmas, Easter, Whitsun) embellish the calendar, and its clergy feel pastoral responsibility towards all who live in their parishes; laws on marriage and Sunday rest, attenuated as they are, and the law on blasphemy prior to 2008, derive from Christian doctrines; charity law specially privileges the advancement of religion (though not specifically of Anglicanism or of Christianity in general); and Christian culture informs the national culture and character. Since all these are public matters, it is by no means the case that religion in Britain is confined to the private sector; Charles Taylor (2007: 1) is wrong to dismiss the remaining connections between Church and state as 'so low-key and undemanding as not really to constitute exceptions' to the separation between them.

Some of this might be changed. The Anglican Church might be disestablished, though not only successive Chief Rabbis but Muslim leaders have defended the established church on what seem to me the spurious grounds that having an official state church raises the profile of religion in society, and that that is good for religions generally. Whether or not that is true, I believe that the automatic appointment of Anglican bishops to the legislature ought to be dropped. Anglican bishops, as well as other faith leaders, can still be appointed (or elected, if an elected chamber is decided upon) in the light of their individual contributions to the public good; what should cease is the *automatic* appointment of clergy of *any* religion to the legislative body.

The impact of Christian culture, rather than Christian doctrine, on British (and for that matter American) life today is pervasive, by which I do not mean to imply that it is a bad thing, but just that it should not be overlooked. I am reminded of what Karl Marx wrote in 1844 in his diatribe against Bruno Bauer and the Young Hegelians, with reference to the imposition of Sunday as the day of rest in secular French schools:

> Now according to liberal theory, Jews and Christians are equal, but according to this practice [of having the public schools open on Saturday but closed on Sunday], Christians have a privilege over Jews, for otherwise how could the Sunday of the Christians have a place in a law made for all Frenchmen? Should not the Jewish Sabbath have the same right? (Marx and Engels 1956: 155)

However, the abolition of Sunday as the principal day of rest in Britain, or the institution of the Jewish Saturday or the Muslim Friday as alternatives, would generate considerable legislative and social disruption, and should certainly not be undertaken lightly. The current pragmatic approach, whereby businesses that remain closed on the Jewish Sabbath are exempted from some provisions of the Sunday laws, seems more sensible, but should other faith group require similar accommodation this would surely not prove difficult.

Secular government, i.e. secularity as opposed to secularism, allows religious voices to be heard in the public space, and religious views to be considered by the administration. Religious bodies and individuals, after all, have as much right as others to expect their views to be heard. But there are two limitations:

1. They should not be specially privileged over other groups and individuals.
2. They should argue their case on a humanitarian (ethical and scientific) rather than a doctrinal basis. For instance, opponents of early abortion should be expected to produce scientific evidence to persuade others that an embryo is as fully developed a human being as its mother, and therefore entitled to equal protection, rather than arguing on doctrinal premises or on the basis of scripture, *halakha* or *shari'a*. Such argument presupposes the possibility of rational ethics independent of religion, a topic which lies at the heart of Enlightenment intellectual concern, and to which John Rawls, Jürgen Habermas and others made distinguished contributions in the late twentieth century in the context of public policy.

As it happens, Jewish and Islamic views on abortion are similar, though very different from those of Roman Catholics. In other matters we may differ from each other or even among ourselves. Governments need to be aware of such differences. Jews, in my experience, have often argued as to who should represent them to the government, and I have noticed that the same sort of disputes occur among Muslims. Jews tend to think that Jews must always speak with a united voice, and many Muslims think that Muslims should always speak with a united voice. I believe this is a mistake. We should not be afraid to admit that there are many kinds of Jews, and many kinds of Muslims, and there is no one Jew or Muslim who can speak for all his or her coreligionists. Also, there is a danger, especially with ideologically-motivated representatives, that it is the most strident who are heard and who are wrongly thought of as typical of the communities to which they belong; we have to make sure that our silent majorities are heard too.

Is there a conflict between Islam and the West?

Abdullah Sahin writes,

> A major *external* dynamic influencing contemporary Muslim self-understanding is what was once known as the struggle between Islamdom and Christendom, which, after a profound secularisation process, has come to be termed as the Islam–West conflict. (p.4)

He is clearly uncomfortable with this characterisation, and with good cause, for the notion of a systematic confrontation between East and West, or between Islam and Christendom, is misleading and damaging.

True, many Islamic countries have only recently emerged from a period of domination by the West. But that was itself preceded by some centuries in which Islam held a lead, culturally as well as politically, from which it was only slowly dislodged. We all have errors to acknowledge, and not only in the past.

More profoundly, what the world is witnessing is a *general* movement from earlier models of religion and the kinds of society that were built on those models. This movement affects Judaism, Christianity and Islam equally, and indeed precedents might be sought under the Abbasid Caliphate in Iraq or in al-Andalus, though it was in the early modern period in the Christian West that such secularizing tendencies took firm root, a process well described in works such as Charles Taylor's (2007) *A Secular Age*.

In essence, the shift is a move away from a world of absolutism, where it was generally accepted that religious leaders (priests, rabbis, imams) were in possession of the final truth on everything that mattered, to a world where a good deal of ignorance is acknowledged, and where knowledge is seen as something acquired gradually, falteringly, and through collective effort, rather than through divine revelation to prophets – where a prophet is an inspirational figure and a moral guide, and not a major source of information about the world. Society is no longer structured as a hierarchy, with men in possession of the ultimate truth determining how everyone should behave; democratic models prevail, and the authority of priests and hereditary rulers wanes.[1]

The tension is therefore *not* primarily between Islam and Christianity or Islam and the West, even if by some historical accident there might, at this time, be an 'Islamdom' majority on one side and a 'Christendom' majority on the other. It is a *universal human struggle* to adjust to what is loosely called 'modernity', and people of all faiths are equally involved.

Traditional religious leaders find this development threatening, and not without reason, since it certainly undermines their authority and deprives them of the opportunity to control society in the ways in which they did for so many centuries. Among their followers, some feel insecure, and seek security by turning to more extreme, 'fundamentalist' interpretations of their faith, while others are quite happy to be able to shrug off the more onerous aspect of religion or to abandon it altogether in favour of secularism. Abdullah Sahin has accordingly characterized the Muslim response to recent developments as twofold:

1. A strong *reactionary traditionalist* perspective
2. An equally categorical *secularist-modernist* position

But this is precisely what has been happening within the other faith communities. That is why it is so valuable for us to engage in dialogue with each other as well as with the secular administration; we all need to discover how to relate to the modern world without abandoning our distinctive community relationships.

---

[1] Whether Taylor's characterisation of our society as the 'Age of Authenticity', i.e. of fulfilment of individual potentiality, is apt is not a matter I can consider here.

Can religion be reduced to values?

Abdullah Sahin has urged that Muslims should draw on traditional Islamic values, particularly that of *ijtihad*, which he understands as critical engagement, to engage in dialogue with Western secular democracy. 'Sustained cultural engagement', he observes, demands considerable skill.

There are two issues I should like to raise here. First, how are Islamic values to be defined, seeing that Islam is so complex and varied a tradition? There can, of course, be no simple answer to this. Islam has sacred texts, schools of interpretation and four major schools of law (just within the Sunni strand of Islam). It is certainly possible to discern within the sources of Islam elements of what are seen in the West as liberal, enlightened values, but it is also possible to find texts or interpretations that are intolerant, discriminatory or unduly restrictive. The *scholarly* aspect of this question can be settled easily – yes, of course, it is possible to discern within the sources of Islam elements of what are seen in the West as liberal, enlightened values; some of them, arguably, arose within Islamic societies. The *practical* aspect of the question is more difficult. How can Muslim communities ensure that these are the values that are *actually* promoted in their midst (who controls preaching, or what is taught in the *madrasa*?)?

My second question is whether it is really possible to *reduce* Islam, or for that matter any of our traditional religions, to a set of ethical and moral values. Abdullah Sahin's citation of the principle of *amr bi'l-mar'uf wa nahy 'an al-munkar* ('commanding good and forbidding wrong') is analogous with Moses ben Nachman's ('Ramban', 1194-1270) citation of 'You shall do what is upright and good in the eyes of the Lord your God' (Deuteronomy 6:18) as a governing principle in the determination of the law. I cannot speak for Muslim jurists, but certainly Ramban and the Jewish jurists never intended that the principle of doing good and shunning evil was a *full* articulation of Torah, for surely there is far more to religion than ethical and moral values. There are quite specific laws (*halakha*, *shari'a*), rituals, history, legends, spiritual exercises and a whole vocabulary shared by the faithful and which articulates their relationships with God, with each other and with the world. It is this which makes each faith group distinctive. Often enough it is these specific aspects of the religious life which impinge upon public space, and a balance must be struck between the desire for distinctiveness as a religious community and the need for coherence in society as a whole.

Where Secular and Religious Values Conflict

The equal status of women before the law is perceived by traditionalists in some religions as an attack on their values. British society has, however, developed to a point where there is a strong consensus for equality, and legislators can insist on this, at least in the public sphere. Some countries with institutionalized churches, for instance Sweden, have insisted on equality of the sexes within the churches, to the extent that women should have equal rights to the priesthood. This is the wrong solution to a dilemma of government; far better to disestablish a Church than for government to interfere in matters that touch church doctrine.

Social groups vary considerably in their attitudes to relations between the sexes, and to the use of alcohol and other mind-altering substances. This is often the real cause of friction between communities, though the communities themselves may deny this and mislead sociologists into looking for other causes. Indeed, the demand for denominational schools stems in large part from such considerations; religious parents are reluctant to expose their children to the sexual freedom and substance abuse that they believe they would meet if allowed to mix freely with the non-religious. In my experience, such issues prove far more deeply divisive than relatively superficial but headline-attracting matters such as whether Muslim girls may wear veils in school or Christians may sport crucifixes or Jewish boys may keep their heads covered.

Reason and Religion

Dr Sahin noted that whereas 'secularity should not be thought of as a rejection of religion,' secularism 'places scientific rationality at the heart of the humanistic endeavour and additionally insists that reason ought to supersede religion'. There is indeed a kind of secularism that, it seems to me, relates to true liberal and democratic ideals in much the same way as extremist religion relates to true faith: it is a distortion and a parody. But this is no reason to reject scientific rationality, provided that scientific rationality is not allowed to run away with itself and make pronouncements about matters beyond its reach; religion and science must, indeed, respect each other, take care not to invade each other's sacred turf, and not be afraid to learn from one another. Unfortunately, it is not easy to know where one turf ends and another begins.

I conclude my remarks with a fulsome endorsement of Abdullah Sahin's conclusion: 'The public and therefore political space, informed by the values of justice, respect and tolerance, holds the clue to perpetuating an egalitarian and just social order' (p.13).

References

Marx, K. and F. Engels (1956) *The Holy Family or Critique of Critical Critique*, trans. R. Dixon and C. Ditts (Moscow: Foreign Languages Publishing House).

Taylor, C. (2007) *A Secular Age* (Cambridge, MA: Belknap Press).

Chapter 4

∾

Towards a critically-faithful
Muslim presence in public decision-making
A rejoinder to Spencer and Solomon

Abdullah Sahin

I would like to begin this rejoinder by thanking both Nick Spencer and Rabbi Norman Solomon for their thoughtful reflections on Chapter 1 and for raising several important issues. Their response suggests broad agreement with the main argument of Chapter 1 that *secularity*, unlike the narrower and more ideological concept of *secularism*, can be interpreted as a crucial inclusive principle informing modern democratic political order and should not be seen as inherently in conflict with or a threat to religion. The diverse models of secularity within Western liberal democracies suggest that, alongside other value systems, faith traditions are recognised and their collective claims and sensitivities can be, to varying degrees, accommodated. The remainder of the paper developed an Islamic socio-political theology that encourages a *critically-faithful* Muslim presence, which entails active engagement within the framework of secular democratic politics, and that is committed to preserving human dignity, and upholding values of socio-economic justice and the common good.

In his response, Nick Spencer draws attention to the complex processes of public reasoning within the secular system and the crucial role of socio-political institutions that mediate public decision-making. It is undeniably the case that this process is not free of power politics and does not always function in a neutral and egalitarian manner. However, the very fact that the secular system facilitates public discussion strongly reflects its inclusive character. As such, I agree that what is crucial is the 'participation of religious people', and that the active presence of a religious voice in such debates may have an influence upon the outcome of many public policy decisions. Given their histories, it is unsurprising that Christianity and Judaism were both constitutive of and are therefore acclimatised into the Western secular democratic system and that they do, to a certain degree, retain some influence on public policy. However, the situation of Islam, their sister faith, is not so straightforward. In fact the legitimacy and relevance of Islam still remain in question. Moreover, there are those who argue that Islamic teachings are essentially in conflict with the values of secular liberal democracy. Therefore, the European Muslim diaspora is perceived to pose a real threat to secular liberal democracy itself.

In the more flexible British model of secularity, visible markers of Muslim identity in the public sphere – such as accommodation of Islamic dress code, dietary requirements and interest free banking, coupled with the incorporation of consent-based resolution of disputes in accordance with the *shari'a* under the Arbitration Act of 1996 – can be seen by some as indicating the gradual Islamisation of the system itself. Moreover, the fear of a home-grown terrorist threat increases mistrust between Muslims and the wider public. Under these admittedly challenging conditions, if the secular state takes an assimilationist turn, instead of treating Muslims as fully-fledged citizens and encouraging civic engagement and participation, then the outcome may well lead to greater isolation. Let me stress that this isolation would not be a matter of formal rights as such but more one of public legitimacy and reputation. This potential marginalisation, coupled with the realities of an unresolved post-colonial trauma that are still with us, creates the conditions in which attitudes of rejection would even lead a few to declare Britain as illegitimate and unworthy of loyalty. However, while one can see how such mutually-exclusive and prejudicial attitudes could develop, an ethic of more self-critical reflection would foster strategies of engagement that would promise more responsible, convergent, and, most crucially, shared ways forward.

There is no space here to explore adequately the ongoing debate over how best to combat extremism and radicalisation in Britain. However it is a good illustration of the urgency with which we need to address serious challenges that concern us all in ways that are mutually self-critical and therefore allow us to converge upon collective solutions. There are legitimate grounds to criticise aspects of the government's counter-terrorism strategy (see Birt 2009, Kundnani 2009), but, nevertheless, it is unfair to put all the blame upon the secular state, as its public decision-making process on the issue did not entirely exclude the Muslim community which has, on the whole, been somewhat lax in claiming ownership of the problem and in articulating clearly the boundaries of healthy and mature Muslim religiosity so that unhealthy extremism could be identified and combated. Instead of an honest and rigorous critical engagement, it seems that political pragmatism, implicitly endorsed by self-proclaimed 'Muslim leaders' and by politicians, continues to influence public policy on the issue significantly.

Apart from the distinct sensitivities presented by the case of Islam, cultural plurality in today's globalised world does pose new challenges to Western secular democracies that have so far largely emphasised secular neutrality and political inclusion within their respective nation-state boundaries, notwithstanding the alternative laic (French republican), legal separation (American) and accommodative (British and north-west European) models noted elsewhere in this volume (Chapters 5 and 8). As such, the meta-narrative of secularity needs genuine rethinking, considering the new reality of greater religious diversity in the twenty-first century. While this is a daunting task that cannot be realized overnight, achieving just representation and broad equity within this context of greater plurality poses serious challenges to public decision-making. A wider diversity of values inevitably adds new challenges alongside the more familiar conflict of interest that animates politics in a more culturally-homogenous democracy.

Both Nick Spencer and Norman Solomon rightly draw attention to the fact that scientific and technological rationality dominates public reasoning within the public space created by secularity, often at the expense of religious viewpoints. However, in my view, so long as competence in human communicative reasoning is not reduced to only one of its instances, i.e. the scientific mode, then developing an insider's understanding, appreciation and recognition of each other's life-worlds and respective sensitivities will remain a necessary and desirable feature of secularity. Indeed, to the extent that democratic channels of communicative rationality are kept alive, as critical theorists such as Jürgen Habermas suggest (Habermas 1986, Habermas and Ratzinger 2007), then a more broadly-shared and just public sphere can be sustained. Finally, it should be stressed that scientific rationality, while it is esteemed because its strong evidential character qualifies it to claim objectivity, it cannot in itself always guarantee a just ordering of priorities in multicultural societies where there may be marginalised others. Thus, it is not only the exercise of instrumental rationality but also a moral competence to reach out to the other that demonstrates the strength of humanitarian and civilizational forces within society.

As I argued in Chapter 1, Qur'anic scriptural reasoning itself strongly reflects Divine trust in humanity's inherent ability to use reason to arrive at just and truthful resolutions of conflict-laden social and political issues. It is therefore unsurprising to see that during the formative development of

Islamic intellectual disciplines, Muslim scholars recognised the open-ended nature of Islamic epistemology; namely, that it is centred on exercising socially-responsible, collective and expert processes of reasoning, as is evident in several passages of the Qur'an (e.g., 4:83). The foundational sources of Islam, the Qur'an and *Sunna*, are brought to bear upon new life situations by novel reflection through the mediation of analogy (*qiyas*), taking into consideration the public interest (*maslaha*) and a host of other social and intellectual tools that lead, historically speaking, to the institutionalisation of *ijtihad*.

The Qur'an, as argued in Chapter 1, in many instances explicitly encourages the application of a creative hermeneutics to resolve social disputes in a realistic and morally-competent manner. In making allowance for a considerable degree of human agency, the process of *ijtihad* should not be misconstrued as limiting God's sovereignty (*hakimiyya*) over creation. Indeed, within the Qur'anic worldview, human responsibility and a certain degree of freedom are firmly recognised, given the central challenge made by God to humanity to choose a life of faithfulness and good conduct (18:7; 67:1-2). The theological debate around what has come to be known as *hakimiyya* is not explicitly explored here and neither was raised by my respondents. However, I hope that my theological argument has already demonstrated that the active presence of human agency in politics should not be taken as contradicting God's sovereignty. It should be stressed that there is often a considerable degree of misunderstanding about certain Qur'anic passages that are too easily taken as pointing towards a God-centred socio-political governance that leaves little space for human agency. For example, the Qur'anic passages that warn the 'People of the Book', and particularly the Jews of seventh-century Madina, against ignoring the Divine guidance they already possessed and neglecting its authoritative application to their lives (5:44-45), have been constantly subjected to a naïve hermeneutics and are used to declare the illegitimacy of a modern secular and democratic state. However, addressing the wider issues that have informed the emergence of such hermeneutic simplicity goes beyond the limits of this rejoinder.

Rabbi Solomon rightly warns us of the danger that a secular system can pose to the narrative integrity and historical continuity of faith traditions, or to the totality of their life worlds, reducing them to an ethical or a value dimension that is less publicly visible and is therefore deemed less threatening. There is a degree of truth in this observation. However, it should be clarified that what I meant by the concept of 'value' in Chapter 1 was not merely an isolated cognitive category containing some abstract virtues or ethical doctrines but rather what constitutes the core of faithfulness as rooted in a specific faith tradition. It should be noted that considered within its indigenous historical context in Western Europe, secularity emerged precisely because religion had lost its capacity to manage the diversity and dynamism to be found in human life equitably. Indeed if religious creativity is reified in ritual and in historic institutions then the danger remains that this impulse cannot be meaningfully applied to confront new challenges. What is crucial is to keep alive those values that created these historic institutions in the first place. Ironically some interpretations of today's liberal democracy have reached a similar position vis-à-vis the values underpinning its principle of secularity – what was originally meant to be an inclusive principle is now in danger of becoming reified and reduced to a rigid ideological attitude, secularism, that resists the inclusion of a faithful other.

The principle of inclusive secularity within liberal democracy may be a blessing in disguise for the future of Islam in Britain as well the larger European and indeed Western contexts. In fact, secularity may well prove to be a necessary part of preserving both individual human rights as well as the sensitivies of collective identities and their survival in an increasingly plural society. While this radical plurality inevitably creates conflicts of interest, the real test is whether our respective cultures and religious traditions will provide arguments that will inspire the making of a shared, just society and will produce exemplary practical leadership in so doing. Within today's radical plurality, one is obliged to show humility by acknowledging the limits of one's own identity politics. Nurturing critical openness remains vital too in facilitating genuine reciprocity and dialogue. Both humility and openness, I strongly believe, will inspire the emergence of genuine solidarity, respect and recognition in order to bring about more meaningful ways of being and living together.

References

Birt, Y. (2009) 'Promoting Virulent Envy? Reconsidering the UK's Terrorist Prevention Policy', *RUSI Journal*, August, 154/4: 52-8.

Habermas, J. (1986) *The Theory of Communicative Action (Vol. 1: Reason and the Rationalisation of Society)*, trans. by Thomas McCarthy (Cambridge: Polity).

Habermas, J. and Ratzinger, J. (2007) *Dialectics of Secularisation: on reason and religion* (San Francisco: Ignatius Press).

Kundnani, A. (2009) *Spooked! How not to prevent violent extremism* (London: Institute of Race Relations).

Part II

Political Perspectives

Part II

Political Perspectives

Chapter 5

∼

Civic Recognition and Respect for Religion in Britain's Moderate Secularism[1]

Tariq Modood

One of the features of the 'cultural turn' in social studies and of identity politics is that, while many think one or both may have gone too far, it is now commonplace that the classical liberal separation of culture and politics or the positivist-materialist distinctions between social structure and culture are mistaken. Yet religion – usually considered by social scientists to be an aspect of culture – continues to be uniquely held by some to be an aspect of social life that must be kept separate from at least the state, maybe from politics in general and perhaps even from public affairs at large, including the conversations that citizens have amongst themselves about their society. This religion–politics separationist view, which is clearly normative rather than scientific, can take quite different forms, either as an idea or as practice and can be more or

---

[1] This chapter is largely based on two previous papers, 'Moderate Secularism, Religion as Identity and Respect for Religion', *The Political Quarterly*, 2010, 81/1:4-14, and 'The struggle for ethno-religious equality in Britain: the place of the Muslim community' in M. Higgins, C. Smith and J. Storey (eds.) (2010) *The Cambridge Companion to Modern British Culture* (Cambridge: University Press), pp. 296-314.

less restrictive, I shall call 'secularism'. While acknowledging the variety of forms it can take I want to argue that one of the most important distinctions we need to make is between moderate and radical secularism. The failure to make this distinction is not just bad theory or bad social science but can lead to prejudicial, intolerant and exclusionary politics. I am particularly concerned with the prejudice and exclusion in relation to recently settled Muslims in Britain and the rest of Western Europe but the points I wish to make have much more general application.

The chapter has three parts. Firstly, I argue at an abstract level that it does not make sense to insist on absolute separation, though of course it's a possible interpretation of secularism. Secondly, radical separation does not make sense in terms of historical actuality and contemporary adjustments. This includes a consideration of how British Muslims operate more widely within the sphere of modern democratic identity politics. Thirdly, given that secularism does not necessarily mean the absence of state–religion connections, I explore five possible reasons for the state to be interested in religion.

Radical and moderate secularism

If secularism is a doctrine of separation then we need to distinguish between modes of separation. Two modes of activity are separate when they have no connection with each other (absolute separation); but activities can still be distinct from each other even though there may be points of overlap (relative separation). The person who denies politics and religion are absolutely separate can still allow for relative separation. For example, in contemporary Islam there are ideological arguments for the absolute subordination of politics to religious leaders, as say propounded by the Ayatollah Khomeini in his concept of *vilayat-i-faqih* (governance of the jurist), but this is by no means a consensus among the different schools of Islamic thought. Historically, Islam has been given a certain official status and pre-eminence in states in which Muslims ruled (just as Christianity or a particular Christian denomination had pre-eminence where Christians ruled). In these states Islam was the basis of state ceremonials and insignia, and public hostility against Islam was a punishable offence (and sometimes a capital offence). Islam was the basis of jurisprudence but not positive law. The state – legislation, decrees, law enforcement, taxation, military power, foreign policy, and so on – were all regarded as the prerogative of the ruler(s), of political power, which was regarded as having its own imperatives, skills, etc., and was rarely held by saints or spiritual leaders. Moreover, rulers had a duty to protect minorities. Similarly, while there have been Christians who have believed in or practised theocratic rule (e.g. Calvin in Geneva) this is not mainstream Christianity, at least not for some centuries.

Just as it is possible to distinguish between theocracy and mainstream Islam, and theocracy and modern Christianity, so it is possible to distinguish between radical or ideological secularism, which argues for an absolute separation between state and religion, and the moderate forms that exist where secularism has become the order of the day, particularly Western Europe, with the partial exception of France. While radical secularism has been adopted by certain states (e.g., Soviet Union, China, Turkey) it is not the mainstream version amongst democracies, even if some democracies have radical aspects, such as the contemporary interpretation of the 'wall of separation' clause in the US Constitution. In nearly all of Western Europe there are points of symbolic, institutional, policy, and fiscal linkages between the state and aspects of Christianity. Secularism has increasingly grown in power and scope, but an historically evolved and evolving compromise with religion is the defining feature of Western European secularism, rather than the absolute separation of religion and politics. Secularism does today enjoy hegemony in Western Europe, but it is a moderate rather than a radical, a pragmatic rather than an ideological, secularism. Indeed, paradoxical as it may seem, Table 1 shows mainstream Islam and mainstream secularism are philosophically closer to each other than either is to its radical versions.

*Table 1: Islamic and secularist views regarding the
separation of religion and the state*

Religion–State	Radical Secularism	Radical Islam	Moderate Secularism	Moderate Islam
1. Absolute separation	Yes	No	No	No
2. No separation	No	Yes	No	No
3. Relative separation	No	No	Yes	Yes

Is British secularism accommodative or ideological?

Having established at an abstract level that mutual autonomy does not require separation I would like to take further the point that I have already begun making that while separation of religion and state/politics is a possible interpretation of secularism, it does not make sense in terms of historical actuality and contemporary adjustments. Most of Western, especially North-Western Europe, where France is the exception not the rule, is best understood in more evolutionary and moderate terms than an ideological characterisation of Western secularism. They have several important features to do with a more pragmatic politics; with a sense of history, tradition and identity; and, most importantly, there is an *accommodative* character which is an essential feature of some historical and contemporary secularisms *in practice*. It is true that some political theorists and radical secularists have a strong tendency to abstract that out when talking about models and principles of secularism. If this tendency can be countered, British and other European experiences cease to be inferior, non-mainstream instances of secularism and become mainstream and politically and normatively significant, if not superior to other versions.

Accommodative or moderate secularism, no less than liberal and republican secularism, can be justified in liberal, egalitarian, democratic terms, and in relation to a conception of citizenship. Yet it has developed an historical practice in which, explicitly or implicitly, organised religion is treated as a public good. This can take not only the form of an input into a legislative forum, such as the House of Lords, on moral and welfare issues; but also to being social partners to the state in the delivery of education, health and care services; to building social capital; or to churches belonging to 'the people'. So, that even those who do not attend them, or even sign up to their doctrines, feel they have a right to use them for weddings and funerals. All this is part of the meaning of what secularism means in most West European countries and it is quite clear that it is often lost in the models of secularism deployed by some normative theorists and public intellectuals. This is clearer today partly because of the development of our thinking in relation to the challenge of multicultural equality and the accommodation of Muslims, which highlight the limitations of the privatisation conception of liberal equality, and which sharpen the distinction between moderate or inclusive secularism and radical or ideological secularism. I have in my work expressly related the accommodative spirit of moderate secularism to the contemporary demands of multiculturalism (Modood 2007).

I would argue that it is quite possible in a country like Britain to treat the claims of all religions in accordance with multicultural equality without having to abolish the established status of the Church of England, given that it has come to be a very 'weak' form of establishment and the Church has come to play a positive ecumenical and multi-faith role (Modood 1997, Parekh 2000: 257-61). Some other relevant considerations are nicely captured by John Madeley in his characterisation of an important strand in contemporary antidisestablishmentarianism:

> a residual opposition to and prejudice against what is seen as the unnecessary destruction or removal of those sets of arrangements, which have been found in many parts of Europe to make for the accommodation of religious diversity. It is not a doctrinal or ideological '-ism', more a rationalisation for a particular brand

> of cultural conservationism, which does not like to see old land-marks unnecessarily done away with and claims they are not to be valued as mere heritage but because they actually serve useful purposes ... virtual quasi-establishment. (Madeley 2006: 404)

There is nothing in this that necessarily jeopardises equality of respect. Indeed, in approaching the reform of institutions, multiculturalists should be particularly sensitive to the ways that the historical and the inherited can be valued in a variety of ways, including giving people a sense of belonging and national identity.

Faced with an emergent multi-faith situation or where there is a political will to incorporate previously marginalized faiths and sects and to challenge the privileged status of some religions, the context-sensitive and conservationist response may be to pluralise the state–religion link rather than sever it. This indeed is what is happening across many countries in Western Europe (Modood and Kastoryano 2006). In relation to the British case one can see it in a lot of incremental, ad hoc and experimental steps. For example, some years ago Prince Charles, the heir to the throne and to the office of Supreme Governor of the Church of England let it be known he would as a monarch prefer the title 'Defender of Faith' to the historic title 'Defender of *the* Faith' (Dimbleby 1994: 528). As Grace Davie has said,

> the affirmation of diversity as such is not a new idea in British society; what is new is the gradual recognition that religious dif-ferences should be foregrounded in such affirmations. Paradox-ically, a bastion of privilege such as the monarchy turns out to be a key and very positive opinion former in this particular debate. (Davie 2007: 232-3)

If such examples are regarded as merely symbolic then one should note how British governments have felt the need to create multi-faith consultative bodies. The Conservatives created an Inner Cities Religious Council in 1992, chaired by a junior minister, which was replaced by New Labour in 2006 with a body with a much broader remit, the Faith Communities Consultative Council. Moreover, the new Department of Communities and Local Government, which is represented in the Cabinet, has a division devoted to faith communities. Or better still, consider an example of a high level proposal (not yet acted on and may not be acted on) which combines the symbolic and practical at a constitutional level, namely the recommendations of the Royal Commission on the Reform of the House of Lords (2000). It argued that the Lords, the U.K. upper chamber, should have 'the ability to bring a philosophical, moral or spiritual perspective to bear.' It believed that it was time to end the hereditary principle of membership of the House but it did not recommend a wholly elected chamber. It thought that its ideals would be better met if part of the House continued to be unelected. The latter includes one of the elements of 'establishment', namely the right of 26 Anglican bishops to sit in the Lords. The Royal Commission endorsed this principle but argued that the number of Anglican bishops should be reduced to 16 and that they should be joined by five representatives of other Christian denominations in England, five seats should be allocated to other Christian denominations in the rest of the U.K. and a further five should be used to include the presence of non-Christians. Hence, they sought to make up the democratic deficit that arises when national fora are completely dominated by party politicians by not just proposing an increase in the width of religious representation but also in the number of seats from 26 to 31.

Such proposals might be regarded as a form of reforming or pluralizing establishment without abolishing it. It suggests that 'weak establishment' can be the basis for moving towards 'multicultural equality' without constitutional disestablishment (cf. Bader 2003 and 2007). I am not contending that some version of establishment (weak or plural) is the only way or the best way of institutionalizing religious pluralism in Britain or similar countries. My point is that a reformed establishment can be one way of institutionalizing religious pluralism. In certain historical and political circumstances, it may indeed be a good way: we should be wary of ruling it out by arguments that appeal to what has been misleadingly called 'the dominant and defensible western versions of secularism' (Bhargava 2006: 93), which simply means trying to be more like France or the US. Stronger still: such institutional accommodation of minority or marginal faiths runs with the grain of mainstream Western European historic practice.

British Muslims and the struggle for ethno-religious equality
While I will discuss below the reasons why the secular state might continue to be interested in religion, intrinsic to how the secular state might accommodate minority or marginal faiths is the assessment of how the claims these groups make are understood and characterized. I will briefly outline how the claims of religious groups ought to be seen within the context of Anglo-American equality movements (for more detail, see Modood 2005 and 2007).

Britain has long been a multi-faith society that is characterized by an internal plurality which has been supplemented by the migration of different religious groups over the last two centuries (Filby 2007). The most recent and numerically significant addition to this plurality include those Hindus, Muslims and Sikhs who have arrived through processes of chain migration, family reunification and social reconstruction over a period of 50 years. Indeed, these former Commonwealth citizens have now established themselves, with varying degrees of success, as part of the 'new cultural landscape' of Britain (Peach and Gale 2003).

Simultaneously, the presence of these new population groups has made manifest certain kinds of racism to which anti-discrimination laws and provisions may not be geared to redress. Initially influenced by American thinking that took the grounds of discrimination to be that of 'colour' rather than ethnicity or religion, religious-minority assertiveness only became a feature within these frameworks from around the early 1990s. Prior to this, the racial equality discourse of British equality movements were dominated by the idea that the post-immigration issue was 'colour racism'. This led to the idea in the 1970s and 1980s that all potential victims of 'colour-racism' should be conceived of as a single 'black' group though it is doubtful if most South Asians ever shared this view and certainly did not do so by the late 1980s; indeed, for South Asians religious identities seem to be more pervasive than 'racial' ones (Modood *et al.* 1997: 291-7). Nevertheless, one consequence of the official approach is that the legal and policy frameworks still reflect the conceptualisation and priorities of a black-white racial dualism (Modood 2005).

The initial development of racial equality in Britain was directly influenced by American personalities and events. Just as in the United States the colour-blind humanism of Martin Luther King Jr. came to be mixed with an emphasis on black pride, black autonomy and black nationalism as typified by Malcolm X, so too the same process occurred in the UK. Indeed, it is best to see this development of racial explicitness and positive blackness as part of a wider socio-political climate which is not confined to race and culture or non-white minorities. Feminism, gay pride, and the revival of a Scottish identity are some prominent examples of these new identity movements which have become an important feature in many countries, especially those in which class politics has declined in salience; the emphasis on non-territorial identities such as black, gay and women is particularly marked among Anglophones. In fact, it would be fair to say that what is often claimed today in the name of racial equality, again especially in the English-speaking world, goes beyond the claims that were made in the 1960s. Iris Young expresses well the new political climate when she describes the emergence of an ideal of equality based not just on allowing excluded groups to assimilate and live by the norms of dominant groups, but on the view that 'a positive self-definition of group difference is in fact more liberatory' (Young 1992: 157).

This significant shift takes us from an understanding of 'equality' in terms of individualism and cultural assimilation to a politics of recognition, to 'equality' as encompassing public ethnicity. In this political and intellectual climate what would earlier have been called 'private' matters, such as personal relationships and sexual orientation, had become sources of equality struggles. It is in this American-inspired climate that religious minority assertiveness emerged as a British domestic political phenomenon quite different from the US. At least in Britain, the advances achieved by anti-racism and feminism (with its slogan 'the personal is the political') acted as benchmarks for later political group entrants. While religious minorities raise distinctive concerns, the logic of their demands often mirrors those of other equality-seeking groups and can be framed in terms of political multiculturalism (Modood 2007).

Why the secular state might be interested in religion

Having then established that the separation of state and religion is neither a necessary feature of secularism in terms of abstract logic nor in terms of mainstream practice, and that the claims of religious identity movements can be accommodated within secular politics as claims to equality, I would now like to consider some of the reasons that the state might be interested in religion. I leave aside state attacks on religion, such as those by the Jacobins, the Soviet Union, or Communist China, that are characteristic of totalitarian secularism. I shall confine myself to democratic examples and to affirmative reasons. I offer here five types of policy reasons in a typology of my own devising. The issue I am exploring is: what kind of reason is a particular proposal or institutional purpose appealing to, what distinguishes it and what kind of legitimacy might it have? I am not arguing that these lines of reasoning lead to obvious policy results – that would require a much greater degree of contextualisation than I offer here – and I am not here trying to determine policies. While I appreciate of course that all actual cases can consist of a mix of reasons, my typology of reasons is as follows:

1. Truth
2. Dangerous
3. Useful
4. Identity
5. Worthy of Respect

I shall discuss them in this order but will give most attention to the last two, religion as identity and respect for religion.

1. Policy based on Religion as Truth

If we consider 'policy' here to mean the state as a whole, i.e., as a holistic structure, then the idea that it is based on a putative truth as understood by a religion, is clearly not compatible with democracy and certainly not a democratic multiculturalism. This is not necessarily because it is religious but because it is a totalitarian ideology; the same would apply to totalitarian secularism. As is the case with Plato's ideal republic based on the truth as understood by a philosophical Guardian, such totalitarian states would also fail to respect the autonomy and integrity of either politics and/or of religion.

There is a real sense, as Plato noted, that democracy is based on opinions not truth. Having said that it does not follow that there may be no scope for truth. Consider the famous statement from the US Declaration of Independence (1776):

> We hold these truths to be self-evident that all men are created equal, that they are endowed by their Creator with certain inalienable Rights, that among these are Life, Liberty and the pursuit of Happiness.

This truth however was not reiterated in the Constitution (1787) itself and so is at least one step removed from specific policies and laws, similar to as I earlier suggested most Muslim-majority states have and do conceive of the relationship between Islam and the state, namely as foundational rather than in terms of positive law.

What about specific policies that are alleged to be based on religious truth, for example, policies relating to abortion or genetic engineering? I am not sure but in principle such policies probably would be acceptable if the policy proposal was subject to a democratic process, was implemented within a framework of individual rights and allowed for exemptions on grounds of conscience.

So specific policies based on religious truth are probably compatible with democracy and multiculturalism, but in any case some of the remaining ways in which policies relate to religion are compatible. So of any proposal based on 1, we might want to ask is it justifiable by reference to any of the others below?

Just as we can do physics without having a view as to whether God exists, so similarly the state may not have a view on whether God exists or whether any religion is true. But that does not mean that the state is not interested in religion.

2. *Policy based on Religion as Danger*

This might seem odd to include here as I had said I was only interested in 'affirmative' reasons. I include it because where religion in general or a particular religion or a particular aspect of a religion is thought to be dangerous and in need of state control – because for instance otherwise social peace or unity is at serious risk – control might mean supporting favoured religious institutions. We see this in the case of how one of the most intolerant (semi-)democratic secular states, Turkey, has a whole government department, the Diyanet, devoted to propagating, funding and staffing a particular version of Islam. The French state does something similar in relation to versions of Catholicism, Protestantism and Judaism and is trying to do the same with Islam (Bowen 2007). The British government has for some years been seriously considering whether and how it needs to be involved in the training of imams, and on a more dramatic scale, had to work with Catholics and Protestants, clerics as well as others, in order to end political violence in Northern Ireland. While the Catholic Church and the Protestant Churches were strong enough to resist manipulation by government or political activists, Muslims in Britain have much less organisation and status to resist pressures by the state – or radical corpuscles – who try to shape a religion according to their own political agenda. Hence there is always a danger of a moderate secularism, whose goal, while mindful of the relative mutual autonomy of politics and religion, is the inclusion of organised religion into the polity slipping into a radical statist secularism.

My general point is that you do not have to think religion is benign in order to support it or interact with it; support and interaction involves regulation anyway.

3. *Policy based on Religion as Utility*
Religion may be a very personal thing but it can produce social outcomes, some of which may be desirable or undesirable in the view of the state and so it might wish to encourage or discourage religion. For example, suppose it were true that religious people are less likely to commit crime or less likely to have a marriage breakdown, with all of its attendant problems, that may be regarded as a reason to encourage the relevant religion regardless of whether one believed in it or not oneself. Some people have believed that whilst adults can do without religion it nevertheless is pedagogically important. That it may be a good way to inculcate morals because it provides an imaginative scaffolding for moral precepts, or assists the development of the imagination in general (Collingwood 1924: 124-5). A research project I have been involved in shows that amongst young British Pakistani working class males there are high drop-out rates from school but they are less amongst those who say they practise Islam (Shah, Dwyer and Modood 2010; cf., Modood 2004). So, any of

these may be, at least hypothetically, reasons for the state to support religious institutions in the hope that, however indirectly, certain outcomes would follow that would lessen the scale of certain social problems and reduce the cost of remedies to the public purse.

More directly the state may observe religious organisations as serving the needy – the poor, the aged, the homeless etc. – either just within their own communities or more generally and these may be economical ways of providing certain services which the market could not provide and which the state could provide less economically or with more political difficulties. So the state may choose to fund these religious organisations.

4. *Policy based on Religion as Identity*
This may work in relation to identity at a number of levels.

A. INDIVIDUAL IDENTITY
For example: I am an X (e.g. a taxpayer) and so want Y (e.g. a certain kind of school). The same identity appeal can be generalised: We are X and so want Y.

B. PUBLIC OR CIVIC IDENTITY
This may refer to an identity as a polity or a country: We are a Christian country and so Christianity should be taught in schools or be referred to in the constitution and so on. This does not have to be a particularly conservative argument. The same logic is present in the following: We are no longer a Christian country and have to re-make the national identity to reflect new inclusions, or we need to have multi-faith schools or a plurality of schools within the state system and reflected in the national curriculum.

C. MINORITY IDENTITY
The state may note that certain religious groups and identities are stigmatised and as with other kinds of stigmatised, marginalised or oppressed minorities, there may be a project to turn these

negative identities into positive ones. This could include (i) anti-discrimination in relation to religious groups and (ii) even-handedness in relation to resources. Where one or some religions, perhaps for historical reasons, have a certain status or certain provision then these may need to be made available to the previously absent or excluded minority faiths too. This can be done without strict 'equality'. For example, as the leading Anglican prelate, the Archbishop of Canterbury crowns the British monarch. Other faiths could be invited to share in this ceremony in some way without necessarily all having the same grand role. In other cases, one might judge even-handedness required granting a special status to some religious groups but not to the population in general. This could be an exemption such as those enjoyed by the male, turban-wearing Sikhs in Britain in relation to the laws on motor-bicycle helmets and 'hard hats' on building sites.

Moreover, one can imagine that some special provisions may be created for a minority as a disadvantaged group, perhaps even without there being a corresponding provision for the majority faith. For instance, in Britain certain advisory and consultative bodies have been created in relation to Muslims but not other religious groups because it is perceived that Muslims have certain problems (e.g. 'radicalisation') that others do not have. This is comparable to the fact that we have a Minister for Women but not a Minister for Men. Another example would be that in March 2008, Britain repealed the blasphemy law, which only related to Christianity, because of the general feeling, shared by many Christians, that it did not need this protection, while an offence of religious hatred has been created because of a perception of vulnerability on the part of some minorities (although technically Christians are covered by it too).

It should be noted that minority identity protection or recognition can apply not just where the majority is of one religion but also where it is non-religious. Some people seem to think that if there is not one populous religion then there is an absence of hegemony or domination, but there could be a secularist or even an anti-religion hegemony in relation to which a minority provision may be sought.

i. *Criterion of inclusivity*

Just as we sometimes use gender, race and ethnicity as criteria to test the inclusivity of an institution (e.g., a workplace, a university or a legislature) so it may be thought appropriate to use religious identity. Just as a civil service under-represented by female managers might need a remedial policy so similarly it might need to a policy to address the under-representation of Muslims in senior posts. The issue is not confined to numerical presence but crucially extends to the symbolic remaking of public/common/national identities, of the 'We' referred to in 4(B) above. Minority religious identities may need to be explicitly recognised in our sense of what the country is and will be in the future. This is about minorities such as Muslims as co-citizens and worthy of respect as co-citizens, it is not in any way an endorsement of a particular religion such as Islam (that would be the first case, policy based on religion as truth).

ii. *Dialogue/Multilogue*

The whole process of minority identity recognition should be dialogical, or more precisely, multilogical, because there are many parties and all are entitled to speak. That is the way of finding out about identities, negotiating compromises, the remaking of new identities and so on but also of identifying the problems and discussing and finding solutions.

Someone might be opposed to minority identity and recognition for a number of reasons and I would like to address one, namely that minority identities are decomposing and becoming privatised and so the kind of identities needed for recognition or accommodation are not available. Actually, I draw on this sociology myself and while I think it complicates recognition I don't believe it kills it off (Modood 2007).

In his seminal essay 'New Ethnicities', Stuart Hall (1992) argued that there has been a shift from taken-for-granted, singular cultural, ethnic and collective identities to self-conscious identities – the 'innocent black subject' is a thing of the past (if that). People are active in identity formation; indeed, racial and ethnic identities are not merely ascribed, they are a form of agency in all senses of the term. Interestingly, this means, though Hall did not draw this implication, that a commonly-drawn contrast between race as ascription and religion as choice no longer holds.

Not only are these identities impure, hybridic, fluid and varied but for some their significance will be *associational* rather than merely or primarily *behavioural*. For example, in the Fourth National Survey of Ethnic Minorities, virtually everybody with an ethnic minority background said their ethnic identity was important to them and large majorities said their religious identity was important to them but some of these individuals did nothing distinctively 'ethnic' in behavioural or 'religious' terms (Modood *et al.* 1997: 334-8). This can have policy implications, e.g., while about 50% of Muslims wanted Muslim faith schools within the state sector, only half of these individuals said they would send their own children to one if it was available locally (in 1994). This may not be just about abstract fairness. Some Muslims can see their own identities in some ways as negativised, i.e., there is something wrong with Muslims. Some kind of sentiment such as 'Most Muslims are problematic but you are OK!' It blocks the way for the 'OK Muslims' too for they may think, 'If that is the way you think about Muslims or if joining you is joining that view then I cannot join you.'

Olivier Roy has applied this kind of sociology to Muslims internationally. He suggests that Muslims, especially younger Muslims and those in the West, are much less likely than their parents or previous generations to do or believe things just because it is the done thing in their faith community (Roy 2004). They are less likely to be customary or conventional or obedient

Muslims but to think about and question what it means to be Muslim and to come up with their own answers, and which may radically vary amongst themselves as well as with customary or authoritative Islam. I think this is right but calling it 'individualisation', as Roy does, is quite misleading, for in some contexts that is seen as a corollary of 'privatisation' and 'secularisation'. These identities are not private. Increased personal and associational agency is a constitutive feature of these identities and the questions being asked by the relevant individuals – What does it mean to be a Muslim? What kind of a Muslim am I? – typically are open to public projections of identity commitment and contestations. What is at stake are indeed public identities and so contemporary British and other Muslim assertiveness can at least partly be understood in terms of identity politics and accommodated within a civic multiculturalism and existing secularist institutional accommodation of religion.

5. *Policy based on Respect for Religion*
There is an image of religion as organisations or communities around competing truths, which are mutually intolerant, which perhaps even hate each other's guts. There is some truth in that in some times and places but the opposite is more important. Let me illustrate this by reference to my late father, a devout and pious Muslim (M.S. Modood 2003), coming to the view that I should attend the daily Christian non-denominational worship at my secondary school. When I told him that I could be exempted from it, like the Jewish children, if he sent in a letter requesting this, he asked what they did during this time each morning. When I told him that some read comics, some took the opportunity to catch up with homework and some even arrived late, he said I should join the assembly. He said that as Christians mainly believe what we believe I should join in fully but whenever it was said that Jesus was the Son of God, I should say to myself, 'no, he is not'. It is a view that can perhaps be expressed as it is better to be in the presence of religion than

not and so the value of religion does not simply reside in one's own religion. One's own religious heritage is to be cherished and honoured but so are those of others and the closing down of any religion is a loss of some sort.

I would suggest that historically it has been a prevalent view in the Middle East and South Asia, indeed where respect for the religion of others has extended to joining in the religious celebrations of others, borrowing from others, syncretism and so on (e.g. Mazower 2006, Nizami 1974). It is something that the West (where mono-religion has been the historical norm) can certainly learn from, as I think some people of my generation realised and which is evidenced in the interest in the spiritualities of 'the East'. Respect for religion does not however require syncretism. It is, however, clearly beyond toleration but also utility for this valuing of religion and respect for the religion of others, even while not requiring participation, is based on a sense that religion is a good in itself, is a fundamental good and part of our humanity at a personal, social and civilizational level: it is an ethical good and so to be respected as a feature of human character just as we might respect truth-seeking, the cultivation of the intellect or the imagination or artistic creativity or self-discipline not just because of their utility or truth. We can think religion as a good of this sort regardless of whether one is a believer or not just as we can think music or science a good whether I am musical or scientific or not. A person, a society, a culture, a country would be poorer without it. It is part of good living and while not all can cultivate it fully, it is good that some do and they should be honoured and supported by others.

This view could be part of Religion as Truth but is not dependent upon it or any kind of theism for it can be a feature of some form of ethical humanism. I think it can be justified within a philosophy of human plurality and multi-dimensionality of the kind to be found in for example R.G. Collingwoood's *Speculum Mentis* (1924) or Michael Oakeshott's *Experience and its Modes* (1933).

Respect for religion is, however, clearly more than respect as recognition or recognition of religious minorities, and, while I am mainly concerned to argue for the latter, I am open to the former, especially as I believe that respect for religion is quite common amongst religious believers (the mirror-image of Richard Dawkins' view that religious people are inherently antagonistic) and I worry about an intolerant secularist hegemony. There may once have been a time in Europe when a powerful, authoritarian church or churches stifled dissent, individuality, free debate, science, pluralism and so on but that is not the present danger. European cultural, intellectual and political life – the public sphere in the fullest sense of the word – is dominated by secularism and secularist networks and organisations control most of the levers of power, and so respect for religion is made difficult and seems outlandish but may be necessary as one of the sources of counter-hegemony and a more genuine pluralism. Hence, respect for religion is compatible with and may be a requirement of a democratic political culture.

I appreciate that this may seem to be, and indeed may be a form of 'privileging' religion. For in this idea that the state may wish to show respect for religion I am going beyond not just toleration and freedom of religion but also beyond civic recognition. Nor am I simply pointing to the existence of overlaps and linkages between the state and religion. The sense of 'privilege' may not however be as strong as it may seem. After all, the autonomy of politics is the privileging of the non-religious, so this is perhaps qualifying that non-secular privileging. Moreover, it is far from an exclusive privileging. States regularly 'privilege' the nation, ethnicity, science, the arts, sport, economy and so on in relation to the centrality they give it in policymaking, the public resources devoted to it or the prestige placed upon it. So, if showing respect for religion is a privileging of religion, it is of a multiplex, multilogical sort, not a singular privileging. Moreover, it is based on the recognition that the secular is already dominant in many contemporary states, and so it is less privileging than compensatory and aimed at furthering not diminishing democratic plurality and civic inclusivity.

In any case, I offer my comments on respect for religion more tentatively than in relation to the other four elements of my typology. We clearly need to separate the five positions out and differentiate between their normative justifications and policy implications but we may still wish to appeal to more than one of them at a time or for different policy measures; or perhaps to appeal to some of them without repudiating the others.

References

Bader, V. (2007) *Secularism or Democracy: Associational Governance of Religious Diversity* (Amsterdam: Amsterdam University Press).

Bhargava, R. (2006) 'Political Secularism' in John S. Dryzek, Bonnie Honig and Anne Phillips (eds.) *The Oxford Handbook of Political Theory* (Oxford: University Press), pp. 636-55; reproduced in G. Levey and T. Modood (eds.) *Secularism, Religion and Multicultural Citizenship* (Cambridge: University Press), 2009, pp. 82-109.

Bowen, J. (2007) *Why the French don't like headscarves: Islam, the State and Public Space* (Princeton: University Press).

Collingwood, R.G. (1924) *Speculum Mentis or The Map of Knowledge* (Oxford: University Press).

Davie, G. (2007) 'Pluralism, Tolerance, and Democracy: Theory and Practice in Europe' in T. Banchoff (ed.) *Democracy and the New Religious Pluralism* (New York: Oxford University Press).

Dimbley, D. (1994) *Prince of Wales, A Biography* (London: Little Brown).

Filby, L. (2007) 'Religion and Belief' in Pat Thane et al (eds.) *Equalities in Great Britain, 1946-2006* (London: Centre for Contemporary British History), pp. 48-65, available at http://archive.cabinetoffice.gov.uk/equalitiesreview/upload/assets/www.theequalitiesreview.org.uk/equalities_in_gb_1946_2006.pdf.

Hall, S. (1992) 'New Ethnicities' in Donald, J and Rattansi, A (eds.), "Race", *Culture and Difference* (London: Sage).

Madeley, J. (2006) 'Religion, Politics and Society in Europe: Still the Century of Antidisestablishmentarianism?', *European Political Science*, 5: 395-406.

Mazower, M. (2006) *Salonica, City of Ghosts: Christians, Muslims and Jews, 1430-1950* (New York: Alfred A. Knopf).

Modood, M.S. (2003) *My Faith and I Rest Here*, private publication.

Modood, T. (ed.) (1997) *Church, State and Religious Minorities* (London: Policy Studies Institute).

——— (2004) 'Capitals, Ethnic Identity and Educational Qualifications', *Cultural Trends*, 13/2, no 50, June, 87-105.

——— (2005) *Multicultural Politics: Racism, Ethnicity and Muslims in Britain* (Minneapolis and Edinburgh: University of Minnesota Press and University of Edinburgh Press).

——— (2007) *Multiculturalism: A Civic Idea* (Cambridge: Polity Press).

Modood, T., Berthoud, R., Lakey, J., Nazroo, J., Smith, P., Virdee, S. and Beishon, S. (1997) *Ethnic Minorities in Britain: Diversity and Disadvantage* (London: Policy Studies Institute).

Modood, T. and Kastoryano, R. (2006) 'Secularism and the Accommodation of Muslims in Europe' in Modood, T, Triandafyllidou, A and Zapata-Barrero, R (eds.) *Multiculturalism, Muslims and Citizenship: A European Approach* (London: Routledge).

Nizami, K.A. (1974) *Some Aspects of Religion and Politics in India during the Thirteenth Century* (Delhi: Idarah-i-Adbiyat-i-Delhi), 2nd edition.

Oakeshott, M. (1933) *Experience and its Modes* (Cambridge: University Press).

Parekh, B. (2000) *Rethinking Multiculturalism: Cultural Diversity and Political Theory* (Basingstoke: Macmillan).

Peach, C. & R. Gale (2003) 'Muslims, Hindus, and Sikhs in the New Religious Landscape of England', *The Geographical Review*, 93/4: 487-8.

Roy, O. (2004) *Globalised Islam: the search for a new ummah* (London: C. Hurst & Co.).

Royal Commission on the Reform of the House of Lords (2000), *A House for the Future* (London: HMSO).

Shah, B., Dwyer, C. and Modood, T. (2010), 'Explaining Educational Achievement and Career Aspirations among British Pakistanis: Mobilising "Ethnic Capital"?', *Sociology*, 44/6.

Young, I.M. (1992) *Justice and the Politics of Difference* (Princeton: Princeton University Press).

Chapter 6

∼

Secular Governance in a Multi-faith Society

Ted Cantle

Many countries, including all Western-style democracies, are now clearly multi-faith societies in which a number of faiths are a valued part of plural society and are enabled to practise and to play an active part in the social and cultural life of their followers, for whom faith and culture are often inextricably linked. For a number of reasons, particularly given the present pre-occupation with the Muslim community, the notion of 'faith in the public sphere' has been taken as any visible manifestation of faith, or the representation of faith-based arguments to further a particular cause, as evidence of its' 'public' presence. Such a limited view is neither practicable nor desirable and the principal concern and focus should be on governance: the extent to which faith organisations influence the organs of the state and, more especially, whether the system of governance is seen to be based upon the views and wishes of one, or more, of the belief systems that underpin them.

The focus on the Muslim community has meant that discussion has revolved around whether one faith has had more privileged access than the others. But the prominence, both nationally and internationally, of the faith debate in recent years has also given rise to a related and equally significant issue: whether faith communities in general have a higher standing in the eyes of government than non-faith constituencies. Furthermore, we also have to recognise that whilst the position of faith is changing, particularly at an international level, so too is the nature and role of the state. In this regard, given the evermore demanding requirements of the modern democratic framework, decision-making processes will have no legitimacy unless they are based upon evidential standards that no belief system can meet, whether or not it is faith-based.

There is a general confusion about what is meant by 'secularism', with most definitions revolving around a separation of church and state, without any real clarity about the nature of that division. Tariq Modood in Chapter 5 usefully attempts to move us on from the notion that secularism is a 'doctrine of separation' to more nuanced divisions based on 'radical' and 'moderate' models. Various attempts have been made to define 'secularism', which are generally broadly-based and contested notions of the way in which the society and culture become detached from religious doctrine and influence (see for example Berger 1969). Parekh (2009) also reminds us of the early usages of the term, which relied upon the notion of the contrast between the 'immanency and time-boundedness of the modern world with the atemporality and eternal nature of the heavenly'. There is also no clear and accepted definition of what is meant by faith in the 'public realm' and a recent book devoted to the subject, (Dinham et al 2009) recognises the many different components of the subject. For the most part, the notion of 'faith in the public realm', seems to be more about its surprising 'political revitalisation' (Habermas 2007), at a time when its decline seemed inevitable as science and rationality appeared to have become ever more dominant parts of democratic debate. Terms like 'public realm', 'public square' and 'public sphere' have been used synonymously. The 'public' nature of faith has, for some, been associated with its visibility and, moreover, unfortunately linked with the Muslim community in public policy terms.

I want to argue that the notion of a 'secular society' is simply inappropriate, it can no longer be applied to modern multi-faith and democratic societies and could not, nor should not, be seen as a desirable policy objective. However, there is a real and pressing problem about the salience of faith-based arguments within democratic institutions and decision-making processes, and 'secular governance' is both necessary and inevitable.

The shape and nature of societies has changed profoundly over the last 50 years or so, as a result of population movement, the globalisation of trade and business, the ease and affordability of international travel and communications, as well as impact of conflict, war and climate change (Cantle 2008). Modern democracies have become much more dynamic multicultural and multi-faith spaces. This does not mean, of course, that the dominant faith in any country has entirely lost its position of relative power and influence and has generally been protected by its historic position, often being granted formal status and constitutional privileges as well as being embedded into the social and cultural life of all citizens, for example, through institutional involvement in public ceremonies and the timing of holiday periods. However, such societies now experience many more public influences both from within and without national boundaries.

The emergence of multi-faith societies does not, though, create entirely new problems for a number of states have had to deal with longstanding divisions and conflicts between at least two principal faiths and have generally devised some form of pragmatic accommodation. In the UK, the division between Catholics and Protestants has been evident for 500 years. Elizabeth I, who 'would not open windows into men's souls' when asked if the state should investigate which of her subjects were crypto Catholics, created the first such accommodation – in other words, she upheld the principle of freedom of (religious) conscience from state interference. Yet part of the overall 'accommodation' meant that Anglicans, in the form of an established Church, retained a limited but privileged position over Catholics which has lasted until the present day.

The discrimination against Catholics has endured generally because of its relatively minor nature – royal lineage, representation in the House of Lords and so on – while discrimination in employment and other areas of life were largely dealt with some time ago. But the inherent unfairness and obvious injustice nevertheless remains a source of complaint and is still being addressed, for example, through the proposed reform of the House of Lords.

Given its historic position, the UK, like many other Western democracies then, may have been expected to have had greater difficulty in coming to terms with the emergence of many other faiths, which has been accompanied by the growth of diaspora communities. Again, diaspora communities are themselves not entirely new (Soysal 2002) and the UK, in common with many other European countries, has had a Jewish community – perhaps the longest-standing diaspora – for at least 800 years. But as Jonathan Sacks (2007) has pointed out, the modern diaspora communities have far more significance and they find it easier to sustain themselves than ever before, largely because of the ease of modern transnational communications (Cantle 2004). Any modern system of governance, then, not only has to take account of intra-society pressures from faith and cultural groups, but from diaspora communities who transcend national boundaries and command support at many different levels. In other words, even those societies that have relatively small faith-based minorities and where the majority faith is clearly predominant in the public sphere, they are still effectively influenced by a multi-faith global culture.

As societies have become more dynamic and diverse, so they have inevitably become multi-faith. However, whilst diversity of culture is generally seen as bringing new, interesting and enriching experiences, there is more ambivalence about the diversity of religion, which may be seen as creating more challenge in areas that still have a sacred and sacrosanct basis. This is understandable in the sense that faith is a 'zero sum game', i.e. that one cannot be a member of two faiths simultaneously, and so faith-based belief systems are therefore, by definition, irreconcilable with each other.[1] Nevertheless accommodations have been made and are continuing to develop. Models of co-existence are now prevalent with the emphasis on dialogue and exchange at the cultural level and mutual respect and understanding at the faith level. This approach has recently been endorsed by the British government, following consultation with faith and other bodies in *Side by Side* (DCLG 2008)

But culture and faith are not easily separable. Ratcliffe (2004) illustrates this with particular regard to the way in which the Muslim faith 'transcends the public–private divide, being intrinsic to the way a Muslim lives her/his life.' Ideas about what constitutes religious dress varies from place to place, reflecting cultural sensibilities and, more profoundly, interpretations of religious texts whether they are literalist or adaptive to context. No clear dividing line is possible and even within nation-states the diversity within religious communities is as significant as it is between those of differing ethnic and faith-based groups (iCoCo 2008). The outsider's view of minorities has often confused notions of race, religion and culture, sometimes out of ignorance and sometimes deliberately so. The far right across Europe has propagated the idea that Muslims are a problem community, partly as a means of developing a racist agenda and taking advantage of the lower level of protection given to religious minorities as compared with racial groups.

---

[1] However, non-faith-based systems of belief may be compatible with each other in the sense that holding a fundamental belief about the way the economy might be run, for example, does not amount to a complete belief system, and so there is room for other large areas of agreement.

The discussion about the role of faith in the 'public sphere' (or realm or square) is complex, with perhaps an 'ideal' notion developed that we simply have to return to a separation of state and church, that is,

> one in which citizens have full freedom to pursue their different values or practices in private, while in the public sphere all citizens would be treated as political equals whatever the differences in their private lives. (Malik 2002)

An unfortunate and simple interpretation of the public nature of faith is taken to mean whether faith is 'visible', through the display of religious symbols, like the displaying of the cross, the wearing of the skull cap, or the various forms of head and face coverings for women. This is perhaps the most obvious form of public manifestation, but it is hardly central to the real issue of governance. The UK has long since taken a different view about such symbols, in contrast to countries like France, and they are generally valued as expressions of diversity and seen as part of culture and heritage alongside other forms of traditional dress – at least until the recent demonisation of Muslim minorities. In fact, the protection of religious dress in the public sphere had even been brought into legislation to accommodate religious minorities as long ago as 1976 when Sikhs were allowed to wear their turbans rather than crash helmets when riding a motorcycle. Of course, in some recent and perhaps exceptional cases, dress codes are a basis for division, and bans have been introduced on particular forms of clothing or accessories in the apparent interests of safety or communication. But 'faith visibility' through the wearing of particular forms of religious dress in public is not the principal issue in the debate on the role of religion in the 'public sphere'.

It is also too simple to suggest that the issue revolves around whether people of faith should be allowed to enter the public square and express their points of view based upon their religious beliefs or to proselytise on behalf of their faith. In a democratic society, such debate is not only generally free but should also be welcomed as part of free speech, at least within the limitations of 'incitement to religious hatred' and of preserving public order. In the case of incitement to religious hatred, secularists would argue that such protection has, by law or common convention, gone too far and prevents proper and reasonable criticism of religious beliefs. The campaign in 2008 to promote the view that 'there is probably no god, so stop worrying and enjoy your life' through advertising on public buses is perhaps a reaction to this and a reassertion of that right of free speech (although a similar bus campaign has been banned in Italy). In theocratic or authoritarian societies, even the right to practise a particular religion is in doubt and for them the notion of faith in the 'public sphere' will inevitably have a very different connotation.

The central issue for democracies is, or should be, whether the system of governance is based upon any form of belief system, rather than clear and transparent empirical evidence and science. This is irrespective of whether the belief system is one which is based on faith or some other form of moral or ethical code, or the particular beliefs of an individual leader or group. In a modern multi-faith society, governmental decisions require a rational basis and this inevitably militates against those dictated by one or more faiths, which by definition depend upon beliefs rather than evidence. This is also partly because any decision which is based upon the tenets of a particular belief system will potentially conflict with the beliefs of other faiths and groups who have adopted different moral and ethical codes and so an objective and evidenced-based decision is the only means of ensuring equality of power and influence in a modern multi-faith society.

And whilst the belief system of one group (usually the majority group) could be selected over that of others, the effect would clearly be to disenfranchise those of others and become the cause of tension and conflict. Further, to simply express and act upon the belief that one course of action is to be preferred to another is no longer an acceptable justification for a decision. In a modern bureaucratic state, decisions are open to public and legal challenge if they have not been able to demonstrate a legitimatising process and a reasonable evidential standard. For example, they must show that the relevant consultations have taken place and been taken into account, that expected impacts have been considered, and that the evidence forms the basis of the decision. Nowhere is this more certain than in the criminal justice system, where to assert a belief that a person is guilty of a particular crime would be literally laughed out of court, and generally followed by a writ for slander. Whilst the standards expected in the criminal justice system are higher and clearer, those obtaining in the political system are not far behind and are gradually being extended, largely through the process of judicial review and challenge.

None of this is to say that decisions cannot be based upon some notion of right and wrong and that this notion may have been influenced by religious beliefs. For example, the notion of 'thou shall not kill' is embedded in many faiths and widely adopted as a cornerstone of national and international law. It is variously used to support a range of political preferences, for example to oppose capital punishment, abortion and war. But these are no more than statements of general principle and the practical interpretation of these issues are open to widely diverse views and a simple statement of beliefs, however keenly felt, will not provide adequate justification. With regard to abortion for example, to adopt the approach of the Roman Catholic Church would be to deem that virtually all abortions were prohibited. This is clearly not accepted by people of other faiths and no faith and to adopt such a policy would therefore 'privilege' one faith over others. In order to arbitrate between such competing arguments and to avoid accusations of 'privileging', governments have fallen back on rational argument, with the case of abortion, for instance, being based upon the age at which babies can survive outside the womb, the evidence of health impacts on the mother, or other documented benefits and disbenefits. In other words, governmental decisions are based upon an evidential and objective basis.

A modern multi-faith society will inevitably develop notions of universal rights and responsibilities that transcend all faith and belief systems, often as a means of mediating between them. Indeed, faith and belief systems have given rise to many moral and ethical standards that have long since been incorporated into legal systems. However, it is nevertheless difficult to distinguish the moral case from the practical basis in each case. Again, the belief in the sanctity of human life on a moral basis might have guided a number of legal principles, but it also has a practical impact as a form of reciprocal protection – 'killing others is wrong because others may choose to kill me'!

The adoption of moral values that coincide with the beliefs of one or more faiths is not in itself problematic, providing that there is a consensus which can ensure some form of wider acceptability and that it has a rational basis, in other words, that it is not simply an 'act of faith'.

However, even if governments do not base their decisions upon the tenets of a particular faith or belief system, the way in which they engage with faith communities might create the perception of privileged access and therefore of unfair advantage for one faith, or of faiths in general over and above secular bodies. This has certainly been the case in the UK, where even the Church of England has complained about having less access, and therefore influence, than the Muslim community (Wynne-Jones 2006). Similarly, the secularist groups complain that they are discriminated against in the political process because they have more limited access. Perversely, they are now beginning to be treated for consultation purposes as though they were a 'faith'.

The existence of an established church might therefore be a bone of contention, irrespective of whether the established church represents the majority population; any privileged position in terms of engagement will inevitably be seen as discriminatory. It is difficult to believe that such institutional arrangements can persist in multi-faith societies, given the perception of preferential treatment and unfair advantage. Indeed, this has become apparent to the Church of England, with the Archbishop of Canterbury recently indicating his willingness to contemplate disestablishment (Beckford 2008). The level of influence, however, does not depend upon whether a church is actually formally established and can just as easily be dependent upon less formalised processes. For example, the Church of England may have less influence in the UK, despite its constitutional position, compared to the much more pervasive public role of Christian churches in the United States where they do not enjoy established status.

Our system of governance of course also extends to regional and local agencies, including local authorities. And faith bodies have a number of roles, which are connected to government but not necessarily a part of the structures of governance. For example, many such bodies are funded to deliver public services and are thought to be able offer higher standards in this respect as they can utilise committed volunteers and empathise with and understand the cultural sensitivities of their group. However, whilst this is being questioned by the criticism of 'single group funding' (CIC 2007), there is a distinction between service delivery and that of policymaking, albeit a fine one. This is perhaps most evident in the provision made for publicly-funded faith schools. For the most part, the 7000 faith schools in England are bound by pretty much the same constraints as the other 13,000 non-faith, state-maintained schools. They are generally charged with implementing educational policy – and funded and regulated on this basis – rather than determining it. However, at the margins they are able to determine a number of processes, particularly with regard to admissions and to provide religious instruction to students drawn largely from that particular faith community. Whilst the position of faith schools has been maintained and their number extended a little in recent years, particularly to minority faiths, they have also come under pressure to widen access and to promote tolerance and respect for other faiths (Cantle 2001, Runnymede 2008) and have also been made subject to the duty to promote community cohesion (DCSF 2007).

The debate about 'faith in the public sphere' should therefore revolve around the extent and nature of faith in our system of governance, either in terms of the reliance on belief systems as a justification for particular decisions, or whether one or more faiths has a privileged access to, or influence over, the organs of government as compared to other faiths or those of no faith. In a multi-faith society, no single faith or group or faiths should have a constitutional or practical advantage over any other. Inevitably, the principal church will have to be disestablished, even if the mere fact of establishment should not be taken to imply a wholly unacceptable level of advantage, given ongoing reform and historic accommodations over time. Yet, as noted previously, governance in modern democracies has been built increasingly upon rational-legal decision-making, and so policymakers will seek to demonstrate an empirical and scientific basis for their decisions and will find it increasingly difficult to justify them with reference to overtly value-laden systems of belief and, as far as possible, should be seen to strive for value neutrality. In this way, faith-based beliefs will become increasingly incompatible with the system of governance. However, faith will remain very visible in the public domain for the foreseeable future and will continue to be recognised as a valued component of diversity. In this sense alone, no modern democracy can now ever be thought of as 'secular'. And, in most cases, individual believers and faith organisations will continue to play a significant lobbying role for policies that their faith community supports. Yet this tension between deliberative democracy and evidential decision-making will, however, increasingly produce a higher level of challenge and debate, with both opportunities and risks for faith-based organisations.

References

Beckford, M. (2008) 'Archbishop of Canterbury: Disestablishment would not be the "end of the world"', *Daily Telegraph*, 18 December.

Berger, P. (1969) *The Social Reality of Religion* (London: Faber and Faber).

Cantle, T. (2001) *Community Cohesion: A Report of the independent Review Team* (London: Home Office).

––– (2004) *The End of Parallel Lives?: Final Report of the Community Cohesion Panel* (London: Home Office).

––– (2008) *Community Cohesion: A New Framework for Race and Diversity* (London: Palgrave Macmillan).

Commission for Integration and Cohesion (CIC) (2007) *Our Shared Future* (London: CIC).

Department of Communities and Local Government (DCLG) (2008) *Face to Face and Side by Side: A framework for partnership in our multi-faith society* (London: DCLG).

Department for Children, Schools and Families (DCSF) (2007) *Guidance on the Duty to Promote Community Cohesion* (London: DCSF).

Dinham, A., Furbey, R., and Lowndes, V. (eds.) (2009) *Faith in the Public Realm:Controversies, policies and practices* (Bristol: The Policy Press).

Habermas, J., (2007) 'Religion in the Public Sphere', *http://www.sandiego. edu/pdf/pdf_library/habermaslecture031105_c939cceb2ab087 bdfc6df291ec0fc3fa.pdf*, accessed 12th March 2009.

Institute of Community Cohesion (iCoCo) (2008), *Understanding and Appreciating Muslim Diversity* (Coventry: iCoCo).

Malik, K. (2002) 'Against Multiculturalism', *New Humanist*, 117/2: 1-18.

Parekh, B. (2009) 'Foreword' in Dinham et al (eds.) *Faith in the Public Realm: Controversies, policies and practices* (Bristol: Policy Press), pp. v-viii.

Ratcliffe, P. (2004) *'Race', Ethnicity and Difference* (Berkshire: Open University Press).

Runnymede Trust (2008) *Right to Divide?* (London: Runnymede Trust).

Soysal, Y.N. (2000) 'Citizenship and Identity: living diasporas in post-war Europe', *Ethnic and Racial Studies*, 23/1: 1-15.

Sacks, J. (2007) *The Home that We Build Together* (London: Continuum).

Wynne-Jones, J. (2006) 'Drive for multi-faith Britain deepens rifts, says Church', *Daily Telegraph*, 16 October.

Chapter 7

∼

We Don't Do God?
How the liberal-left can rediscover
a more moderate secularism

Sunder Katwala

What is the appropriate public recognition and role of religion in a society of many faiths and none? Tariq Modood's proposal in Chapter 5 to reconstruct a 'moderate secularism' could offer a useful starting point for those seeking the common ground of a shared citizenship at a time when so much of what passes for public discussion of the question of faith and secularism is ill-founded, polarised and potentially dangerous.

Whether those dangers should be taken *too* seriously could be challenged. It is not unusual to switch on Radio 4 in the morning and hear a Bishop of our Established Church arguing with a pro-secularism columnist for our leading left-liberal newspaper over whom can best claim to speak for a now marginalised and oppressed social group. Such jousting might simply be regarded as knockabout public entertainment.

Other developments are more significant, even if they lack the scale of mobilisation of the 'culture wars' that have dominated a good deal of public discourse in the United States, which the constitutional framework has struggled to contain. But we have seen sharp public antagonism over Islam in particular, and an electoral breakthrough in Britain for the fascist far right in the European elections of 2009.

Some social friction is part of a liberal society. Claims made for and against faith touch on deeply-held convictions about the origins of the universe, what it is to be human and the nature of science and art. A large part of the point of a free society is that it can discuss fundamental questions openly, so that we can all form our own views of the good life, and seek to persuade others of the merits of our respective visions. However, as a society, we also share an interest in something else too. The political challenge is how liberal polities deal with deep disagreements and agree the rules by which we share a society. For the most part, our current dialogue of the deaf between faith advocates and evangelical secularists makes no attempt to do this, preferring instead to trade highly ritualised talking points and mutual caricatures so that their opponents become responsible for either the evil done by fanatics in the name of faith or, alternatively, the Godless horrors of the Gulag.

Why 'We Don't Do God' on the liberal-left

We can only change the terms of the debate if we understand the motivations, and fears, of the participants. So, from a secular liberal-left perspective, I want to explore why a good section of it believes that it has a legitimate, principled and perhaps existential reason for resisting the idea that faith can or should have any public role or recognition at all. (This position is held by relatively few elected representatives of left-of-centre parties, but is probably that argued most often and most vocally in broader civic, media and online liberal advocacy.)

This 'Sorry We Don't Do God' argument engages in discussing the public role of faith mainly to explain that religion is essentially the problem; that the sooner everybody could grow out of believing in such superstitious nonsense the better; and that those who must persist in such personal faith should please keep it to themselves and not bring this to the public sphere. Otherwise, we will simply all disagree in a way that will make sharing public space too difficult.

This is strongly felt because of a fear that an historically-settled question is being reopened, and that rolling back the public claims of religion was part of the happy Whiggish evolution of equality and human rights. It is a claim to a secular settlement which requires a good dose of amnesia, when Britain is the sort of secular state where the Prime Minister appoints Bishops who sit by right in the legislature. The major conflagration over the Rushdie Affair caught liberals by surprise. When calls to 'ban the book' were to be answered with an explanation that we just don't do things like that here, it was somewhat embarrassing to be reminded that the blasphemy law on the statute book, dismissed as an irrelevant archaic hangover, had been used in a successful prosecution just a decade earlier.

Still, liberals suggest that the Church of England did not really count, given a public image that borders on agnosticism. That is a semi-serious point. And the strong secularist response is straightforward: it is time to sort out those anomalies by properly secularising the public space. The Blasphemy Law has finally gone.[1] So disestablish the Church and elect the Lords. Reject demands for more faith schools by abolishing all existing faith-based education: we don't want to turn into Northern Ireland, do we?

High-profile protests to restrict cultural expression show that any more accommodative responses could have dangerous regressive consequences, for free speech, the role of women and for recent progress on gay equality. Resisting such calls from Christian, Sikh and Muslim groups can be taken as proof that this is a principled secularism dedicated to equal opportunity: if

---

[1] The offences of blasphemy and blasphemous libel were abolished in English common law in 2008.

it will resist the claims of all faiths for public recognition, what could be fairer than that?

So it is from the very fact of religious pluralism and disagreement that a demand for a faith-free public space is made. The claim that any engagement with faith must increase friction becomes a self-fulfilling prophecy. The only engagement possible on these terms is bound to be one of mutual incomprehension. This in turn strengthens secularist convictions of the importance of holding the line.

Britain's incomplete secularism unsettled

We need to understand what is important and legitimate in this secularist position. Modood demonstrates why the strong secularist position that insists upon removing religion entirely from public discourse as the only possible foundation for democratic discourse in a plural society risks philosophical incoherence. This seeks to set the 'rules of the game' for public discourse in a way that decides definitively the central issue of contention between religious and secular worldviews, although a faith-free public space could still be one possible outcome of such political deliberation.

This suggests too a pragmatic (secularist) argument for rejecting a doctrinal French secularism. Those polities most concerned to protect public space from the encroachment of private faith are often the least successful in doing so. Defining and defending a strict boundary between the state and religion often ends up with religion being much more salient and sharply contested in national politics, as can be seen in the United States and France and to some extent in India too. The soggy accommodationist approach may inoculate against these sharp edges and could prove more successful in protecting secular values in practice rather than theory.

Rebuilding a social consensus around 'moderate secularism' would depend on convincing enough of those of no faith that offering some public recognition for faith does not threaten or encroach on the core values which underpin secularism, but could rather entrench these, while securing consent from those with faith-based perspectives that this offers common ground for a shared citizenship.

Modood's argument is that the British polity has been largely secular, but it has been a moderate, accommodative and hence incomplete secularism. So the spirit of British secularism is perhaps akin to George Orwell's description of a very English social revolution in his famous wartime essay 'The Lion and the Unicorn':

> It will not be doctrinaire, nor even logical. It will abolish the House of Lords, but quite probably will not abolish the Monarchy. It will leave anachronisms and loose ends everywhere, the judge in his ridiculous horsehair wig and the lion and the unicorn on the soldier's cap-buttons. (Orwell 1941:112)

Interestingly, Orwell also foresaw that his socialist England would 'disestablish the Church, but will not persecute religion. It will retain a vague reverence for the Christian moral code.' (Orwell 1941: 113)

That the British tradition is one of evolutionary change could be an argument for muddling on as we are. But muddling on looks ever more difficult. A public settlement on the role of faith need not to be neat, tidy or logical in every respect. But it can only be a settlement if it is understood, and felt, to be broadly fair and legitimate. The core of the problem is that this is no longer the case in Britain. The status quo is challenged from all sides, though a sharp contest between diverse dissatisfactions as to whether it is the loss of our Christian heritage, the threat to secular values, or the public demonization of minority faiths which should worry us most.

Yet there is a paradox here. The reasons why it is necessary to revisit the question of the role of faith may make this the worst moment to do so. A highly antagonised public discourse sees mutual trust in short supply. This could be the very worst moment to attempt to settle the question of the public role of faith. Yet the conversation is happening anyway – and will take place around flashpoints generated by media controversies and court cases to assert incompatible rights (e.g. school uniforms, the right to wear a crucifix to work or to refuse to perform a civil partnership), which generate public discussion in which nobody seems quite sure what principles are at stake or how the rules of the road might balance these.

A new settlement?

This should be a liberal project. Though resistance to any public role of faith is often voiced as a defence of 'Enlightenment values', less attention has been paid to how this same tradition of secular liberalism offers an important foundational argument for engaging in the type of discussion that Modood proposes. This is the democratic and republican case for politics as civic activity, as argued for by Bernard Crick (2005), which is necessary precisely in order to negotiate collectively a peaceful solution where we disagree with each other. The way we talk about faith often exemplifies the retreat of this democratic and republican sense of politics as inherently collective, as against an anti-politics which is only about the insistent articulation of our own demands, without recognising the need to negotiate, compromise and aggregate views given that other people's views differ.

The high principles of mutual respect to underpin any settlement will not be difficult; the hard issue will be to find agreement on where key boundaries should lie. A reformulation of moderate secularism will have to be bounded by a shared commitment to fundamental human rights, and it might now best aim for the broadly equal treatment of all major faiths by the public authorities within this shared commitment. So the current roles of the Established Church might be shared across faiths where that is compatible with human rights of all, and removed where it is not.

This could be attempted through formal disestablishment, replaced by forms of limited co-establishment. In principle, that would provide a coherent 'moderate secularist' settlement. But there are political disadvantages: the public symbolism of disestablishment and co-establishment might well seem too radical for conservatives and too conservative for strong secularists. So Modood's approach, where the traditional role of the Church of England would effectively help to broker a new settlement between multi-faith society and the state could prove a more effective, gradualist approach to a broadly similar goal. There are, however, different dangers here. This should not be 'co-establishment by stealth' if the goal of public legitimacy is to be achieved. The disagreements must be aired and addressed.

Exploring Modood's possible justifications for a liberal polity to recognise faith could help to do this. It does not seem to me that the first possible justification – the claim for religion as 'truth' – is useful to a liberal polity or multi-faith society. (Again, this is a secular principle we honour in the breach, and a Coronation Oath focused on public service than divine provenance might serve better next time.) But a multi-faith coronation ceremony would appropriately offer public recognition of faith in a way that seeks to foster respect for religion as culture and heritage. These 'dignified' aspects of the constitution offer a natural opportunity to do this. Such symbolic recognition of the role of faith in society need not offend or exclude non-believers. For example, oaths with a public function should be offered in secular (and republican) as well as multi-faith versions to better reflect the sense of personal integrity being demanded of citizens.

Recognising faith in these ways would reflect the reality that the liberal state is consistently more culturally and historically situated than is often claimed. It can enable, rather than undermine, the animating liberal belief that we should make substantive choices about the good life for ourselves if there is public support for opportunities to access high culture, sport or heritage that might otherwise be scarce or non-existent. The test of the liberal polity is not that it abstains from all such patronage, because it can take no view at all about what may have value for many, but that it does not seek to dictate the choices that individuals then make in pursuing their own conception of the good life. And we have a history of facilitating and encouraging faith that is compatible with democratic citizenship and that speaks to the public interest in countering extremism.

And, while a moderate secularism can publicly acknowledge and value religion, it will necessarily take a liberal approach to hard clashes over free expression and offence, the right to autonomy and exit, which depend fundamentally on individual consent and which override group rights. Some will think this still privileges the liberal secularist worldview but all major faiths can recognise this as the essential foundation for substantive deliberation, even where there is disagreement about how to apply these principles in practice.

One more difficult test will be faith schools. Most of the secularist liberal-left instinctively opposes faith schools in principle, which is perfectly arguable. However, the abolition of existing faith-based education is inconceivable in practice. Their long history and current scale means that those who would keep them have sufficient democratic voting power to prevent whole-sale abolition. While that remains out of bounds, the argument for denying the creation or funding of Muslim, Hindu or Sikh schools, similar to existing Church of England, Roman Catholic and Jewish schools is untenable on the grounds of upholding basic fairness. The liberal secularist concern for common citizenship might therefore be better directed towards questions of regulating curriculum content and ensuring interaction across schools.

But this particular case reflects that there are no a priori right answers: these are questions to be politically negotiated. In failing to acknowledge that, the strongly secularist left has risked forgetting its own history. A Labour tradition that owed more to Methodism than Marxism should know that there was a religious left as well as a religious right. The failure to offer an engagement with faith is to turn away from allies in substantive causes of poverty, equality, social justice and climate change. So there is an important prize to be won.

But it may depend on the 'excluded middle' making a concerted effort to disrupt the mutual intolerance of those determined to loudly insist on caricatures – either that all religious faith is incompatible with reason, tolerance or compromise or that atheism can have no basis for ethics – needs to be challenged. It is time for a decisive intervention from the 'excluded middle' which knows that a politics of the common good seeking coalitions for a fairer and more equal society must reject siren calls to see uncompromising 'culture wars' come to dominate our own public debate.

It is time for a new humanist-secular and religious coalition of moderates to tell those battling on our behalf to call off the faith-versus-secularism war, for the call to go out: 'not in our name'.

References

Crick, B. (2005) *In Defence of Politics* (London: Continuum), 5th edition.

Orwell, G. (1941) *The lion and unicorn: socialism and the English genius* (New York: Secker & Warburg).

Chapter 8

~

Secularism and Democracy
Some Responses to Ted Cantle and Sunder Katwala

Tariq Modood

I am grateful for Ted Cantle and Sunder Katwala for their comments. There is much in what they say, especially the latter, that I concur with but here I will mention some points of possible disagreement to clarify what I believe the issues are and my own views in respect of them.

Cantle says that 'the central issue for democracies is, or should be, whether the system of governance is based upon any form of belief system, rather than clear and transparent empirical evidence and science.'(p.83) But is this really an either-or? To give an example, what is the evidence for Mao Zedong's powerful aphorism, 'Women hold up half the sky'? Or is it just a belief of the kind that democracies should be leaving behind? Does the same apply to the declaration by the founders of the United States, that 'we hold these truths to be self-evident that all men are created equal'? Society, including how it is governed, is constituted by beliefs like that; indeed, we distinguish between different societies and different forms of governance by beliefs like that (patriarchy or gender equality, aristocracy or democracy) and not only by reference to the place of science.

Cantle goes on to recognise that while law courts must observe standards of evidence, the laws themselves may, I would say must, be based upon some notion of right and wrong (p. 84). He further recognises that these notions and specific decisions based on them may have been influenced by religious beliefs but they must be open to rational argument, to justification and to the creation of cross-cutting consensus. Indeed they must and that is why reason and belief are not as mutually exclusive as he suggests. Beliefs can be reasoned about but, as in my examples of gender equality and equality of human beings given above, our reasoning is based on certain fundamental beliefs. Moreover, such fundamental beliefs are not singular, discrete beliefs but ways of thinking and acting that different schools of analysis refer to as philosophies, ideologies, hegemonic discourses, social imaginaries etc. A court of law has to have some evidence in order to determine who owns a piece of property; but the concept of property (or of 'justice', of the 'individual' or of 'harm') is not based on 'empirical evidence and science'. Such concepts can be reasoned about, as whole libraries of jurisprudence and moral philosophy testify, but they are neither separable from 'belief systems' nor no-go areas for religious people. Cantle would like us to 'strive for value neutrality' but has not explained how governance is possible outside of 'value-laden systems of belief' and so there seems to be no reason for his belief that 'faith-based beliefs will become increasingly incompatible with the system of governance' (p.87).

Turning to institutional matters, Cantle holds that 'inevitably, the principal church will have to be disestablished' (p. 87). As Katwala recognises, the whole thrust of my argument is that there is nothing inevitable about that in a plural society. For such a society which seeks to make the variety of religious citizens as well as the non-religious citizens full and equal members of a multicultural citizenship, the requirement of disestablishment is not obvious but complex and context-sensitive. Katwala is a most sympathetic discussant who wants to take on board my central points while interrogating them for their compatibility with core liberal, secular and democratic values and whether my point of view is capable of generating a progressive consensus. Nevertheless he does risk misunderstanding one of my key points when he says that 'Modood's argument is that the British polity has been largely secular, but it has been a moderate, accommodative and hence incomplete secularism' (p.93). Yes, British secularism is moderate and accommodative but this is not due to an imperfect or incomplete form of secularism but to a distinctive form of secularism. In Chapter 5, I characterised the actually-existing political secularism of Britain and North-Western Europe as accommodative secularism and contrasted it with the better known liberal, US-style and republican secularism of France and argued that the former was not an imperfect (and hence not an incomplete) version of one of the others. Let me state again what I think is necessary to all political secularisms. This is partly to show why I do not believe that non-establishment is an essential feature of political secularism per se; but also in order to address Katwala's point that 'public recognition for faith [should] not threaten or encroach on the core values which underpin secularism' (pp.92-3).

In Chapter 5, I argued that the essential idea of secularism is the *mutual autonomy of religion and politics*; and that this mutual autonomy may be absolute and radical, but it may also be relative and moderate. The secular state has legitimate reasons in regulating the non-absolute autonomy of religion (as well as promoting organised religion and respect for religion as such). What I did not make clear was that a secular state that begins to control or marginalise religion is unlikely to be a liberal democracy because such control will violate the rights of individual believers. Alfred Stepan very nicely and succinctly expressed what the relationship between religion and politics should be in a democracy:

> Religious institutions should not have constitutionally privileged prerogatives that allow them to mandate public policy to democratically elected governments. At the same time, individuals and religious communities, consistent with our institutional definition of democracy, must have complete freedom to worship privately. In addition, as individuals and groups, they must be able to advance their values publicly in civil society and to sponsor organisations and movements in political society, as long as their actions do not impinge negatively on the liberties of other citizens or violate democracy and the law. (Stepan 2000: 43)

He refers to this relationship as one of 'twin tolerations' and it is clear that this mutual toleration between religion and politics is similar to the relative and mutual autonomy of politics and religion. Stepan believes that it expresses a minimal condition of democracy but that it is less than secularism. My own view is that relative mutual autonomy is the core idea not of democracy but of a secularism that recognises organised religion as a legitimate political presence. This may or may not be in a democracy: we can imagine the idea being practiced regardless of the presence of elections. Hence mutual autonomy is more fundamental to the idea of moderate secularism than democracy.

More importantly and relevantly here, non-establishment is not a characteristic of democratic states. We are here not just talking about nominal or very recent democracies: in Western Europe, five of the EU15[1] and nearly all of Scandinavia have established churches (Sweden disestablished the Lutheran church only in 2000) (Stepan 2000: 41-3). So the view, no secularism with establishment seems to be a Franco-American or perhaps just

---

[1] The EU15 was made up of the following 15 countries – Austria, Belgium, Denmark, Finland, France, Germany, Greece, Ireland, Italy, Luxembourg, the Netherlands, Portugal, Spain, Sweden, and the United Kingdom – prior to the accession of 10 new member states in 2004 and two more in 2007.

an American reading of secularism that does not resonate with the actually-existing secularisms of most democratic polities, especially those in North-West Europe. I suggest, then, that we need a conception of 'political secularism' and 'a secular state' that is more empirically based and sociologically apt in that it recognises where power lies. For the fact is that all countries with an established church, at least in North-West Europe, are secular states, and not just marginally so but overwhelmingly so. The mere presence of an established church does not mean religious domination over non-believers or the domination of one church or religion over all others. The truth is that non-religious modes of thinking, communicating and mobilising, non-religious organisations, parties, networks and individuals, non-religious policies and funding programmes dominate all the countries mentioned above in which establishment is a fact. In none of them is organised religion able to challenge the state or the ruling elites on a legal, fiscal or policy matter except in a few marginal cases where the exceptions prove the rule. Where such challenges have taken place in the last few decades, say on abortion or divorce or homosexuality, even if a religious campaign wins a battle, it usually loses the war in the long run.

Moreover, it would be simplistic to suppose that a country committed to no-establishment, like the US is more (or less) secularist than European countries such as Britain. The United States has a constitutional separation of church and state in its first amendment ('there shall be no establishment') but religious mobilisation is a feature of US politics, and it is commonly said of it that no overt atheist can get elected for a major political office. On the other hand, Britain has an established church in England and another in Scotland, and so fails to qualify as a secular state by the most fundamental of US criteria, yet British political culture eschews religion. An indication of the latter is how Tony Blair's press officer, Alastair Campbell, when asked if the Prime Minister prayed with President George Bush during a visit to the White House, replied, 'We do not do God.' When questioned about this, Blair, among the most openly religious Prime Ministers the UK has ever had, said, 'I don't want to end up with an American-style type of politics with us all going out there and beating our chests about our faith' and that while people were defined by their faith, it was 'a bit unhealthy' if it became used in the political process (BBC 2005).

So, secularism in the US finds its most heightened expression (perhaps its only major expression?) in its constitutional arrangements; in this respect Britain falls short, but, by our own secular standards, US politics are saturated by Christian, especially Protestant, concepts and sensibilities, which shape the hopes and fears, the ideals and blind spots of American political culture (*Social Research* 2009). It is as if two quite different social compacts were at work: in the British (and more generally North-West European) case the deal is that the religious majority can have state recognition at the highest level but then they must exercise self-effacement in relation to the democratic process if not public culture as well. While the deal in the US is if all churches can agree to allow a certain limited area of public life as 'religiously neutral' and 'beyond religion', the rest of public life is an open field for religion. American secularism has a parallel with capitalism: the state is deliberately given a limited role so that each individual and company/church may pursue their interest/salvation to the maximum degree. No one church is given institutionalised primacy so that no one's conscience and perception of religious truth risks being slighted, and so initially all Protestants (and ultimately all religions, albeit in a certain Americanised, Protestantised version) are equally free to not just live by their own truth, run their own places of worship, be free to leave them or set up new ones, but may attempt to *lead the nation*, to make the nation in their own image – as long as it is not through establishment. It is not that politics is a no-go area but establishment is not an appropriate means to further religious ends. American secularism, then, is not the depoliticisation of religion but *the rejection of one political method, namely establishment.*

The American way of being secular is to be religious by all means but one.

I will conclude by asking what kind of constitutional politics will best assist us in Britain in achieving a civic multicultural, moderate secularism in which minorities like Muslims can be respectfully accommodated and in which they and everyone else can express respect for other faiths of the kind that I argued for in Chapter 5. Katwala argues that 'muddling on looks ever more difficult' and a more formal 'public settlement' is now needed (p.93). He may be right but I am not convinced. For me the key tasks are that we need to (i) destigmatise public religion and (ii) pluralise the institutional recognition of religion. It is not obvious to me that this can best be achieved through a single major debate followed by a constitutional change. Such a debate may well be very divisive and paralysing; and countries which put a premium on codified constitutions, such as the US and France, are not examples of countries that seem to be handling the politics of religion temperately. I agree with Katwala that we need to appeal to and activate the non-radical secularists and religionists, what he calls 'the excluded middle', but which as I argued with my Table 1 in Chapter 5, I believe to be the broad middle. I believe that kind of political consensus can best be achieved by and for an incremental, experimental politics rather than for decisive, constitutional shifts that can be full of risks.

References

BBC News (2005) 'Blair shuns US religion politics', 22nd March, *http:// news.bbc.co.uk/1/hi/uk_politics/4369481.stm*

Modood, T. (2009) 'Odd Ways of Being Secular', *Social Research*, 'The Religious-Secular Divide', Proceedings of the Social Research conference at The New School, 76/4: 1169-72.

Stepan, A. (2000)'Religion, Democracy, and the "Twin Tolerations"', *Journal of Democracy*, 11/4: 37-57.

Afterword

Maleiha Malik

In popular discussions, there is a widespread assumption that British Muslims reject secularism. The Satanic Verses Affair or the Danish Cartoons incident are presented as part of a wider malaise within Islam and Muslim communities that prevents them from adapting to liberal modernity, which requires a separation of religion and politics. Moreover, following the bombings in New York in 9/11 and in London in 7/7, religion has become a critical issue in discussions about contemporary political violence. This context means that discussions about the place of religion in liberal democracies invariably lead back to the 'Muslim question'. Yet, the high-profile incidents mask a more mundane social reality in which most British Muslims 'muddle along' making realistic compromises between the requirements of their religion and the demands of day-to-day life in secular Britain.

A unique contribution of this volume is that it focuses on secularism in political science literature as well as in contemporary Islamic political thought. The focus on political science, in particular, ensures that theoretical reflection about British secularism takes seriously the 'facts on the ground'. There are two particular areas in which this approach can make a useful contribution: in relation to mapping out the institutional context, as well as in understanding whether, and how, Muslims can be accommodated into public life.

Institutional Secularism

First, a dual focus on both the Islamic tradition and political science facilitates a deeper analysis of the institutional aspect of British secularism, i.e. the way in which Islam can be integrated into an existing constitutional structure which provides for an established Church of England. A political science perspective allows us to understand the nature of a modern multi-faith society, as well as the realistic options for how government can engage with majority and minority religions. An Islamic perspective is also essential because it helps us to understand the full range of internal conceptual resources available to Muslims who wish to enter into political and social relationships with a liberal democratic state and an established Church.

On the question of institutional secularism, it should be possible for Muslims to maintain a genuine diversity of views. As the contributions in this book make clear, Muslims who seek greater inclusion within British political structures will have a number of options about how they might proceed. They could advocate wide-ranging constitutional reform that calls for the disestablishment of one preferred Church in favour of strict equality between the State and all religious groups. Alternatively, Muslims may prefer a 'multi-faith' model by seeking greater inclusion within the existing system of Church–State relations. Some Muslims may feel that they can comfortably participate in the mainstream structure of British political life without a conflict with their religion. For these Muslims, the discussion of Islamic political theology will provide an important justification for their engagement with political and civic society. The contributions in this volume, as well as the work of scholars such as Khaled Abou El Fadl (2004a, 2004b; also Fadel 2004), confirms that the Islamic tradition contains ample intellectual resources with which to engage with secular modernity. More specifically, the Islamic tradition's focus on political virtues such as justice, as well as individual virtues such as compassion, ensures that it can provide a substantial critique of power. This, in turn, provides many Muslims with a strong motivation to be involved in political campaigns for the common good and redistributive justice. This approach can also provide the basis for productive alliances between Muslims and non-Muslim political actors (e.g. trade unions) towards common political goals. It should also be possible for British secular politics to make room for those Muslims in favour of a 'rejectionist' stance. A secular liberal democracy should respect the rights to individuals who choose to isolate themselves from mainstream politics and society, but who respect the limits of the law.

The institutional context within which the 'Muslim question' is debated is critically important. Political processes, and representative assemblies, have a key role to play in this sphere. The debate about how Islam and Muslims can be accommodated into Britain needs to be carried out within mainstream political and legal institutions rather than being relegated to special 'faith' forums. Civic society and the media are also important actors within this process. This procedure is likely to ensure the broadest range of participation in public debate and political negotiations. This technique also has some potential to generate a deeper and more meaningful identification with national and local institutions, in a joint enterprise, that creates social cohesion and sustains a coherent political community rather than a plethora of self-interested splinter groups. Discussions about the institutional place of Islam and Muslims in Britain that are conducted in this spirit may be able to contribute to a sense of belonging on the part of all citizens, which can be effectively hammered out through debate and compromise carried out in the public sphere.

Accommodative Secularism

Second, an approach which focuses on both an Islamic and political science perspectives provides a useful way of exploring the accommodative aspect of British secularism, i.e. whether the state can accommodate Muslims religious practice. Although the Islamic perspective of secularism may generate an abstract theory, it is important that it is related to the actual experience of secularism by British Muslims. On paper it may seem that Muslim social and political values will conflict with secular democratic cultural practice. Undoubtedly, there are high-profile examples of a clash between an Islamic perspective that religion should be a strong presence in the public sphere and the principle of secularism that seeks to limit religion to the private sphere. The attempts to ban or regulate the Islamic veil set up the conflict as a problem of either gender equality or separation of politics and religion. The Salman Rushdie Affair and Danish Cartoons controversy frame the problem as a conflict between Islam and free speech values. These high-profile cases, however, mask a more complex reality. In practice, such conflicts can often be resolved through processes of negotiation, mediation and compromise.

Two examples illustrate the potential for accommodation by both the Muslim community and state authorities. First, the example from the Muslim community is provided by the situation of some Muslims who refused to provide services to blind customers because they considered that their guide dogs were 'unclean'. This scenario has materialised into practical conflicts in a number of situations, e.g. Muslim restaurant owners who refused to allow guide dogs on their premises. More recently, a Muslim cab driver refused to accept a blind passenger with a guide dog because he claimed that his religion considered dogs to be 'unclean'. Licensing laws require all licensed cab drivers to carry guide dogs. Magistrates at Marylebone fined the minicab driver £200 and ordered him to pay £1200 for failing to comply with regulations set out under the Disability Discrimination Act 1995.[1] The specific risk of a conflict between the Islamic belief on the uncleanliness of dogs and the possibility

---

[1] 'Unclean Blind Dog Banned by Muslim Cab Driver', *Daily Mail*, 6th October 2006.

of direct or indirect disability discrimination against blind people was resolved through non-legal mediation and proactive policies. The issue was considered by the Muslim Council of Britain which, after having sought expert advice on the matter, issued a ruling that British Muslims should allow guide dogs to enter taxis and restaurants. This clarification in the position of the Islamic tradition in relation to guide dogs has improved access for blind Muslims wishing to attend mosques for prayer: a Labrador retriever has become the first dog in Britain to be permitted to enter a mosque, acting as a guide for its blind Muslim owner.[2] In this way, a legal requirement to comply with disability discrimination legislation has led to a productive process of reflection by Muslims about their own religious norms and practice. This, in turn, has resulted in the elimination of a conflict with secular equality laws, as well as the transformation of a religious and social norm within the Muslim community.

A second example from the area of Islamic finance illustrates how the state may resolve these conflicts through a process of pragmatic accommodation. At first sight, it may seem that there is very little space for accommodating Islamic values within the UK political and legal system. Yet, the 'facts on the ground' reveal that in some cases this is both necessary and possible. In the UK, the Finance Act 2003 abolished an excessive double stamp duty on mortgages that comply with those Islamic traditions that prohibit the charging of interest. As most UK mortgages involve the house buyer borrowing money, the regime of a double stamp duty on those mortgages that complied with Islamic law was a significant barrier to the development of more widespread home finance for Muslims. The abolition of this penalty by the Treasury has laid the foundation for cheaper mortgages for those Muslims who are unable to buy normal financial products because their faith prohibits it. This legal change could have

---

[2] 'Muslims Break Taboo To Allow Guide Dog Into Mosque', *Times*, 23rd December 2007.

short term results in terms of greater financial stability through making home ownership easier for British Muslims. It should make the mortgage market operate in a fair and accessible way. There are also longer term and more subtle benefits. This type of modest concession can yield considerable and magnified political benefits for minorities. Such moves have the potential to reduce the gap between the experiences of Muslims in their daily and practical lives and their experience of mainstream legal and political institutions. This in turn can encourage the meaningful identification of Muslims with key secular institutions.

In many situations the call of writers in this volume that Muslims should participate actively within secular liberal democracies is possible. Yet, at the same time, secular liberal democracies do limit the range of reasons and justifications that count as 'public reason' and can justify political and legal decision-making. This, in turn, limits the extent to which the public sphere can reflect comprehensive religious commitments. It would be naïve, therefore, to assume that concepts such as the 'common good' or 'dignity for all' can transcend the possibility of genuine conflicts between the Islamic tradition and British secularism. In areas such as attitudes towards gender equality or sexual orientation there will be genuine – and often intractable – conflicts. However, it would be wrong to exceptionalise Islam or Muslims in this context. British secularism will, in these types of situation, raise problems for sections of all the major religions. A number of high-profile incidents illustrate this problem. The 'Catholic adoption agencies' debate led to public discussion about whether organised religion can provide public goods and services without fully complying with the requirements of equality law for gays and lesbians. In *Ladele v London Borough of Islington*,[3] a Christian registrar of marriages argued that a requirement that she should perform a same-sex civil partnership was a violation of her right to freedom of religion under Article 9 of the

---

[3] [2009] EWCA Civ 1357.

European Convention on Human Rights. The Court of Appeal also dismissed Ms Ladele's appeal. The Master of the Rolls, Lord Justice Neuberger, stated:

> Ms Ladele was employed in a public job and was working for a public authority; she was being required to perform a purely secular task, which was being treated as part of her job.

Not only Islam but all the major religions face a genuine dilemma about how to achieve an optimal balance between private belief and public action in a secular liberal democracy.

Concluding Comments

On the one hand, the 'Muslim question' needs to be treated as part of a wider analysis of how religion can be accommodated into contemporary British life. This raises a more fundamental question about whether religious differences can be accommodated into a liberal public sphere that increasingly insists on equality for women, gays and lesbians. This is a problem that is relevant for majority religions such as Christianity, as well as minority religions such as Islam. On the other hand, the 'Muslim question' raises a distinct set of issues for British secularism. The key 'facts on the ground' about British Muslims includes their lack of access to political, social and economic power as compared with other religious groups. Strategies of accommodation of religious difference raise important questions about the redistribution of resources and power between social groups. In this context, religious minorities such as Muslims who lack access to political, economic and social power will be at a serious disadvantage.

In relation to Muslims, an institutional framework for British secularism requires a realistic acknowledgement that not all religious groups are equally placed in their access to political, social and economic power. British secularism also needs to put into place frameworks that reduce the conflict between the private consciences of Muslims and their full public participation. This can be done by taking a reasonable and proportionate approach to what religious differences can be accommodated in the public sphere in order to 'provide space for people to transform their deepest priorities from being a source of self-estrangement into elements of a sense of personal progress.' (Leader 2007: 730)

References

Abou El Fadl, K. (2004a) 'Islam and the Challenge of Democracy', in J. Cohen and D. Chasman (eds.) *Islam and the Challenge of Democracy* (Princeton: Princeton University Press), pp. 3-46.

––– (2004b) 'Reply', in J. Cohen and D. Chasman (eds.) *Islam and the Challenge of Democracy* (Princeton: Princeton University Press), pp. 111-28.

Fadel, M.H. (2004) 'Too Far from Tradition', in J. Cohen and D. Chasman (eds.) *Islam and the Challenge of Democracy* (Princeton: Princeton University Press), pp. 81-6.

Leader, S. (2007) 'Freedom and Futures: Personal Priorities, Institutional Demands and Freedom of Religion', *The Modern Law Review*, September, 70/5: 713-30.

Index

About the Contributors

Yahya Birt is a Visiting Fellow at the Markfield Institute of Higher Education.

Ted Cantle CBE is Professor at the Institute of Community Cohesion (iCoCo).

Dilwar Hussain is Head of the Policy Research Centre, based at the Islamic Foundation.

Sunder Katwala is General Secretary of the Fabian Society. As with all Fabian outputs, the views expressed are those of the individual author rather than the collective position of the Society.

Maleiha Malik is Professor in Law at King's College, London.

Tariq Modood MBE is Professor of Sociology, Politics and Public Policy at the University of Bristol.

Dr Abdullah Sahin is Head of Research and Senior Lecturer in Islamic Studies and Education at the Markfield Institute of Higher Education.

Dr Ataullah Siddiqui is Reader in Religious Pluralism and Inter-faith Relations at the Markfield Institute of Higher Education.

Rabbi Dr Norman Solomon was Fellow in Modern Jewish Thought at the Oxford Centre for Hebrew and Jewish studies.

Nick Spencer is Director of Studies at the public theology think-tank, Theos.